Lindsay Lohan

The Biography

Lindsay Lohan

The Biography

THE SENSATIONAL TRUE STORY OF AN INTERNATIONAL SUPERSTAR

Sarah Marshall

JOHN BLAKE

Published by John Blake Publishing Ltd,
3 Bramber Court, 2 Bramber Road,
London W14 9PB, England

www.blake.co.uk

First published in hardback in 2007

ISBN: 978 1 84454 448 6

British Library Cataloguing-in-Publication Data:

A catalogue record for this book is available from the British Library.

Design by www.envydesign.co.uk

Printed in Great Britain by William Clowes Ltd, Beccles, Suffolk

1 3 5 7 9 10 8 6 4 2

Papers used by John Blake Publishing are natural, recyclable products made
from wood grown in sustainable forests. The manufacturing processes conform
to the environmental regulations of the country of origin.

Every attempt has been made to contact the relevant copyright-holders,
but some were unobtainable. We would be grateful if the appropriate
people could contact us.

CONTENTS

INTRODUCTION

A road sweeper trundles slowly through the quiet streets of Merrick, Long Island, USA. Already, the first leaves of autumn are beginning to block gutters and driveways, creating a blot on an otherwise picture-postcard landscape. A SWAT team of professional gardeners has already been drafted in to clear up any unsightly debris. The taxes in this neighbourhood are high and with good reason. It's 11.00am, and most of the city-working residents are already comfortably settled behind their Manhattan desks responding to the latest urgent memo. Having dropped their children safely at the school gates, glamorous housewives are rushing to meet their lunchtime appointments for the day.

Dina Lohan pulls into her driveway. Her bottle-blonde hair has been scraped back into a ponytail.

Unlike the other women casually ambling across their front patios, there's a sense of determination about her visit. Cautiously, she switches off the engine and yanks on the handbrake. In the back, her three children – Ali, Dakota and Lindsay – are huddled quietly together. Lindsay, the eldest, peers inquisitively from beneath a mop of red hair. This is the first time the family has been home in a long time.

For the past few months, Dina and her kids have been living with their grandparents. Dina left their father in another blazing row. The fight was sparked by her returning home one evening later than expected. The intensity of the confrontation resulted in her leaving and taking the children with her. Now that she is fairly certain her husband is out of town for an extended period, she's decided it is time to come back.

'C'mon,' she says, smiling encouragingly at the kids, 'let's get this stuff inside.' Stepping out of the car, she's suddenly struck by the reality of her situation. The last time she saw this driveway it was with her face pressing into the tarmac. Having packed a suitcase of overnight clothes for her children, she'd stormed out to the car. Michael had taken up pursuit, begging her to stay. Amidst the confusion, she'd fallen and cut her arm. On examining it closely, a small scar was still visible. Her parents had pleaded with Dina not to return home, but she knew she couldn't stay away forever, but Dina had to believe that things might change. She is a fighter as well and she won't give up easily. She thought that perhaps by the time he returned home, things might be different.

As she turns her key slowly in the lock, doubts creep into her mind. Quickly, she banishes them away. It's too late now for second thoughts. An eerie silence hangs menacingly in the air. Followed closely by Ali and Dakota, who are both in her shadow, she tiptoes quietly inside. She then lets out an audible sigh of relief. The house is empty.

Checking her household is still in order, Dina slowly enters each room. Coffee mugs lie scattered across the kitchen work surface. She frowns; Michael always did refuse to load the dishwasher. Finally, she reaches the bedroom she and Michael share. Her eyes dart about the room, before settling upon the door to her en suite bathroom. It's been left ajar. Call it obsessive compulsive, but Dina always did have a problem with the bathroom being on display. 'Old habits die hard,' she says and smiles to herself before reaching over to pull the door shut.

Suddenly, she detects movement. A shadow flits across the window. In a split-second, the handle is pulled from her grasp. 'What happened next was really fucked up,' says Lindsay, later recalling the incident. Before Dina can gauge what's going on, a figure leaps from the shower. It's Michael Lohan.

Screaming, Dina and the children tear down the stairs. 'He came running out of the house,' says Lindsay, still shaken by the memory. 'I got in the car, and Ali and Cody ran into the car, and we all floored it out and drove back to my grandparents' house. We wouldn't go back there. We got rid of that house.'

Four years later, Lindsay Lohan is an A-list Hollywood starlet on the brink of international stardom. On the surface, it's difficult to imagine that her life could be anything less than perfect, but the cute, freckly kid with a troubled home life has struggled hard to reach the top. Having paved her way in the teen market, she's rapidly becoming a respected actress in her own right and, with an estimated annual income of £11 million, merits inclusion in the Forbes Young Celebrity Rich List. But the transition hasn't been easy. Blighted by rumours of drug-taking, eating disorders and feuds with fellow stars, Lindsay Lohan has become a permanent fixture in the tabloids. Her love of parties has landed the fun-loving teen a reputation as a wild child and her love life has been placed under microscopic scrutiny. It's no wonder the tender 19-year-old's health is starting to suffer, with three hospital visits clocked up in the past two years. Add to her woes a twice-convicted father recovering from a cocaine addiction, who seems hell-bent on airing his family's dirty laundry in public, and you have a plot line far more salacious than any of Lindsay's filmscripts. But, with every gossip story printed, public support for the talented actress continues to grow. 'People like Lindsay because she's real,' says her mother proudly. Given her turbulent life story, that's something of an understatement!

1

PICTURE PERFECT

A former Radio City Rockette, Lindsay's mother, Dina Lohan, was no stranger to the world of entertainment. Originally inspired by the Tiller girls in the *Ziegfeld Follies* of 1922, the Rockettes were the world's top precision-dance group and a major US icon. Performing four shows a day, 365 days a year, there were only ever 36 Rockettes at any one time. The competition for a place in the troupe was fierce, and only the cream of the crop would be chosen. Dina also appeared in various television soap operas and performed in several musicals, including *Cats* and *A Chorus Line*. Glamorous and charming, she quickly caught the attention of Michael Lohan, a Wall Street trader of Irish descent who capitalised on his family's multimillion-dollar pasta business.

Having enjoyed his own taste of minor childhood

fame with a part in a daytime drama called *As the World Turns*, Michael would later sell his business to finance and develop Hollywood productions. He was a flamboyant character who loved extravagance. An extremely charismatic man, he could talk his way into (and often out of) any complicated business deal. He believed in first impressions and had always been regarded as a sharp dresser. Genetically, Lindsay was predestined to be a star.

In 1985, the 20-something couple married and, a year later, on 2 July 1986, their eldest daughter Lindsay was born. Both Dina and Michael grew up in Long Island – she was from Merrick on the South Shore, while he hailed from Laurel Springs in the north – so it made sense to settle in the area. The family set up home in Cold Spring Harbor on Long Island's North Shore, a respectable and peaceful neighbourhood. A former whaling village, the area had been popularised by well-to-do New Yorkers in the 1900s and was even home to Louis Comfort Tiffany, the founder of world-famous jewellers Tiffany's. Leafy and spacious, the area was also home to a famous bird sanctuary and woodland conservation area.

Most inhabitants were white middle-class with an annual income of $200,000. It was an area of the type depicted in F Scott Fitzgerald's famous novel *The Great Gatsby*. All in all, it was a nice place to live.

'They had two-acre zoning there,' remembers Lindsay, 'so we had a lot of property!'

Encouraged by her ambitious mother, Lindsay embarked on a modelling career at the age of three. 'My mom knew some people at Ford Models and they were like, "Oh, bring her in,"' says Lindsay. But Lindsay protests that she was never forced into anything by her parents. 'I would beg Dina to bring me. I was really comfortable in front of the camera and it was fun.'

Committed to her daughter's success, Dina would regularly drive Lindsay to New York for auditions. Eventually, all her children would sign up with acting agencies. Dina was fully aware of the hard work and pitfalls a showbiz career could entail, but she had also experienced (albeit on a smaller scale) the buzz of fame and success. She was careful not to push her children; she'd seen too many overzealous mothers go down that route. She would simply present her children with options and guide them accordingly. Michael played no role in suggesting an acting career to his kids; he left all of that to his wife, who seemed quite content with her newfound occupation. Besides, he was often away on business trips brokering yet another big-bucks deal.

At first, Lindsay's progress was slow. While all the other girls were blonde and blue-eyed, she was the only redhead with freckles. 'But I never complained

3

or cried like a lot of the other kids,' she says proudly. Dina remained patient; she knew success very rarely happened overnight. But Lindsay found it harder. Her grasp on time was very different, and a few weeks seemed like an eternity.

After several attempts at hitting the jackpot, the ambitious wannabe became despondent and swore she'd never act again unless she landed her next audition. Dina tried to ignore her daughter's tantrums, but, when the time came for Lindsay to attend her next audition, she couldn't bear to hear the outcome. To her relief, Lindsay got the part. It was a commercial for Duncan Hines.

When the morning of the actual shoot arrived, Lindsay was a bundle of excitement. Incredibly blasé, she skipped through the shoot with the ease of a seasoned pro. 'I remember there was a lot of cake on set and all I wanted to do was eat the cake,' she giggled. Dina was amazed by her daughter's performance. She clearly had a talent on her hands and, as a mother, she had a responsibility not to let it go to waste.

After making an impressive début, the offers of work started to flood in. Lindsay eventually racked up a whopping 60-plus ads, including work for Gap, Wendy's, Pizza Hut and Jell-O. She describes the latter, where she appeared with Bill Cosby, as one of her favourites. 'We got to laugh and sing Jell-O songs,' she giggles, now embarrassed by the thought. 'I think the flavour was grape. All my friends really liked that commercial. I looked so cute.'

As Lindsay's workload grew, Dina became increasingly focused on her daughter's career. Inevitably, the two forged a titanium-strength bond that remains to this day, with Dina continuing to manage her schedule. 'My mom's the coolest ever!' says an awestruck Lindsay. 'She's my best friend... she's my idol.'

It was true that, from an early age, Lindsay was desperate to follow in her mother's footsteps and idealised her as a role model. 'It's very hard for me to compare myself to my mom,' she explains. 'If you had to describe someone as perfect, she is perfect. She's beautiful, she has four kids and she's fun.' Admiring Dina's ability to make friends quickly, Lindsay hoped she'd inherit the same charismatic confidence. 'She's very outgoing and spontaneous and it's easy for her to go into any room and talk to people. I guess I'm a little more shy than she is in that sense.'

Today, the relationship is clearly reciprocated, with Dina on hand to assist Lindsay in every crisis she faces. 'We're on the phone ten times a day,' says Dina. 'Lindsay and I have always had this open relationship where she tells me everything — sometimes stuff I don't want to hear! Lindsay is a very open soul.'

Lindsay agreed. 'I'm a second mom. I'm a mom to my mom.'

Often, Lindsay's younger brothers, Dakota and Michael, and her sister Ali, would join their big sister at auditions, enviably watching her career unfold. In one instance, the whole clan appeared together in a Calvin Klein advert. As a friendly gesture, the photographer invited the siblings to pose together for a shot. The clients were so pleased with the outcome, they eventually chose to use it for a national advertising campaign. Quite literally, the Lohans presented a picture-perfect image of the ideal family portrait. Only one person was missing from the picture – Lindsay's father.

On the surface, Lindsay appeared to be living a charmed life. Financially, her family had nothing to worry about and she already had her foot firmly in fame's door. Plenty of other children in the neighbourhood were curious as to Lindsay's frequent trips to Manhattan. Dina was careful not to discuss Lindsay's work in public for fear people would get the wrong idea and think she was boasting. Although Merrick was a great place to live, it was also the kind of place where rivalry between residents is fierce. The last thing Dina wanted for her daughter were enemies. Instead, whenever people asked where the family was off to this time, Dina simply used the excuse of visiting a relative.

It was a shame not all of Dina's problems could be resolved so easily. Behind the fake smiles and feigned happiness, the Lohan family was crumbling beneath the pressure of a tough and often absentee patriarch. Michael's temperament was allegedly one of the factors that caused the eventual breakdown of the marriage. Both parents were strong and opinionated characters, and their relationship had always been stormy. Dina would allege that Michael suffered from mood swings, citing male insecurity as their cause. An astonishing claim in the light of Michael's business acumen and established success.

Lindsay's career was beginning to take up more of his wife's time and, quite simply, Michael felt left out. Whereas in the past Dina had devoted her full attention to her husband, it was now being directed elsewhere. Periods of frequent absence from the household didn't help. He would return home to find furnishings rearranged, ornaments moved and his children two inches taller. The world was changing and Michael Lohan felt increasingly disconnected from it. Frustration bordering on anger was an understandable consequence. Reluctant to play the subservient housewife, Dina gave as good as she got. Residents in the sleepy suburb would often complain about raised voices. 'They would yell and scream a lot,' recalls a former neighbour. 'Everyone on the block knew they had troubles.'

Even before Dina and Michael married, problems in the relationship were apparent. Dina would later allege in court papers that Michael had first attacked her on the night of their engagement. 'He brutally struck me without cause,' she claimed. 'I should have left then but I didn't.'

Another altercation took place on the day of their first wedding anniversary. The police arrived and Michael was arrested. She would later claim he had threatened to kill her. 'He made five life-threatening telephone calls to Dina, threatening to kill her and her father,' said her lawyer Eugene Bechtle in court nine years later.

Finally, when Lindsay was just three years old, Dina found the strength to leave Michael. Back then, before Lindsay's siblings were born, she only had one child to consider. It was much easier to walk away. But Michael wasn't prepared to lose his family without a bitter fight. With divorce proceedings in full swing, the couple ended up in court.

Although it initially came as a shock, Dina shouldn't really have been surprised by what happened next; Michael had never been one to take a fight lying down. While battling for custody of their only child, Michael took matters into his own hands and left with Lindsay.

'My parents were in court and I was taken out of the courtroom by my father,' says Lindsay, now amused by the absurdity of her father's actions.

Dina was infuriated by Michael's recklessness. Ironically, it had been that spontaneous streak that had first attracted Dina to Michael. He wasn't like every other man in the street, and that was exactly why she loved him. Dina knew it wouldn't be difficult to track Michael down. When she finally confronted him about taking Lindsay, he explained that he just did not want to lose his family.

Something in Dina's heart softened. No amount of experience can teach you how to deal with love. Dina was desperate to rebuild her family. Having come this far, she couldn't give up now.

To say Michael and Dina bickered constantly would be unfair. Looking back through her family albums, Lindsay does recall plenty of happier memories. Quite a big kid himself, Michael was a master of invention when it came to keeping Lindsay amused. Often, Dina would chastise him for spoiling Lindsay by showering her with sweets and appeasing her every demand. 'I used to drive my dad's car in the backyard when I was little and sit on his lap – in the grass, because we had a lot of acreage,' Lindsay recalls.

Michael would forever mastermind grand schemes for family outings, presumably designed to bring the clan closer together.

Nevertheless, relations between Dina and Michael were often strained. Dina grew ever more resentful. Their relationship did little to reflect the comfortable home life they'd earned for themselves in one of the most respectable suburbs of New York. The pair were constantly at loggerheads.

Unfortunately, Lindsay often found herself at the centre of the family turmoil. As the eldest child, she felt a weight of responsibility upon her shoulders. Her siblings were too young to understand any of the arguments and were often frightened by the shouting. 'I'm the oldest and anything that went on with my parents when I was younger, I was always the one who kind of gets involved in that.' Michael would often disappear for days at a time leaving Lindsay and her mother distraught with worry.

Although Michael refused to give details of his whereabouts, the truth behind his frequent disappearances quickly became apparent. Dina had suspected that Michael had been coping with a drug problem for quite some time. She urged him to seek therapy but, too proud to discus his problems with a shrink, Michael refused outright. The best Dina could do was to shield her children from the truth.

Inevitably, Lindsay would encounter drugs at some point in her life, but Dina was adamant that it wouldn't be in her own home. One day, while playing with her father's belongings, a young

Lindsay stumbled upon a packet of cigarettes. She hated the smell of them, especially when her dad lit one at the dinner table. As she turned the packet upside down to tip out the contents, a small cellophane-wrapped package fell to the floor. Curious, she unravelled it carefully. Unable to identify the contents, she ran downstairs to ask her mum. When Lindsay produced the tiny packet, Dina immediately snatched it from her. Lindsay knew by her reaction that something must be wrong. She would later realise she'd discovered Michael's secret stash of drugs. 'He was blowing his fucking money away,' she sighs.

But, despite the pain he caused his family, Lindsay couldn't help but forgive her father. Once her anger had subsided, she was simply worried about him. 'I was always a daddy's girl, always close to my dad,' she confesses.

As Lindsay grew older, she would learn to seek security and protection outside the family home. 'My friends were always there for me and they were really cool about it,' she says of the domestic conflict she learned to live with. 'As I got older, I was able to finally say, "Listen, this isn't right."'

For the time being, the Lohans stuck together and presented a united front to the outside world. While Lindsay suffered unhappiness at home, she found escapism in her newfound love of acting. On screen at least, the storyline was taking a more positive turn. Lindsay Lohan was about to break the big time.

2
FALLING INTO
THE TRAP

Anyone who knew Lindsay as a child could see she was a show-off. Lively and vivacious, she loved to entertain and be the centre of attention. 'I used to put on shows for my Barbie dolls, singing Madonna or Paula Abdul,' she giggles. Whenever family friends came to visit, they would always compliment Dina on her charismatic young daughter. In many ways, she took after her mother. Very early on, Dina had exhibited a showbiz zeal, taking great delight in performing for an audience. The veteran entertainer identified a similar streak in Lindsay, only it appeared to be much stronger. Dina was certain Lindsay had a spark, the kind of magic capable of transforming a professional into a superstar. It was the quality she'd hankered for as a child but had never quite achieved. Talent like Lindsay's couldn't be taught; it was embedded from birth.

Eager to capitalise on her daughter's talents, Dina enrolled Lindsay in voice lessons at the age of six. Although her singing career wouldn't blossom until years later, the training provided a good foundation for a career in entertainment. For the time being, Lindsay would concentrate on acting. She was already creating a name for herself on the child actor's circuit, so it seemed silly to spread her focus elsewhere. 'I started with acting first so it made sense to go with that,' shrugs Lindsay.

Ironically, she's never taken an acting class – even to this day. Everything she's picked up has been from experience. Lindsay admits one of her greatest attributes has always been the ability to observe carefully and soak up her surroundings. While other child stars would be screaming loudly and demanding attention, Lindsay would simply sit quietly in the corner and watch her co-stars. That's pretty much been the case her whole career and she's never felt the need to seek formal training. 'I'd consider it if there was something about a character I needed to research,' she says, 'but it's never really been suggested to me. I like to do things organically, just read the script and think of what that character would do in any situation. I think that classes might not be good for me.'

Lindsay had featured in countless commercials, but her first taste of TV glory came at the age of seven. It wasn't quite the glamorous début she'd been hoping for, though. Dressed head to toe in scraps of discarded litter, Lindsay appeared on *Late Night with David Letterman* dressed as a piece of rubbish in a sketch called 'Things You Find on the Bottom of the Subway'. Ten years later, she would reappear on the show as a host, something she couldn't possibly have imagined at the time.

When Lindsay was ten, she won her first regular acting job on America's second-longest-running soap opera, *Another World*. Over the years, the show had been a breeding ground for talent, with past alumni including Morgan Freeman, Ray Liotta and Anne Heche. Lindsay would play the character of Ali Fowler, an illegitimately conceived child faced with the daily trauma of dealing with her mother's turbulent love life. She was actually the third actress to take on the role. Lindsay soon fell into a routine with filming and would spend three days a week on set, with the remainder of her time back at school. The studio was also based in New York, so she could happily live at home.

While filming a TV show was fun, both Lindsay and her mother had grander plans in mind. Although she'd never spoken explicitly about it, Dina secretly hoped her daughter would one day make it big in

Hollywood. Gracing the silver screen in Tinseltown had always been an unfulfilled ambition of her own. As a young girl, she'd fantasised about the romantic lifestyles of legends such as Marilyn Monroe and Audrey Hepburn. During her stint with the Rockettes, she'd even had the honour of touring with Ann-Margret. These were dreams and ideals Dina passed down to Lindsay. She gave her eager daughter plenty of classic films to watch and study in a bid to ignite the same passion.

Lindsay was grateful for Dina's guiding hand. Tentatively, she started testing for bigger screen roles. Her first true taste of stardom arrived when she was cast as the lead in 1997's *The Parent Trap* alongside Dennis Quaid and Natasha Richardson, in which she played identical twins Hallie and Annie. The film was a remake of a 1961 classic starring Hayley Mills, but Lindsay was not at all fazed by the legacy she had to follow. 'I think the original *Parent Trap* is really fantastic, really good. I want to meet Miss Mills but I don't think of this movie as following in her footsteps.'

Casting director Ilene Starger describes the search as the most extensive of her career. 'In addition to the normal process, we hired people to look in schools in Los Angeles and New York,' she explains. 'We saw a couple of thousand girls in about an eight-week period.' In addition, Disney received more than

1,500 audition tapes from young hopefuls. But none of the candidates seemed right for the part.

'Most children are not natural. They act like goofy sitcom children,' complained director Nancy Meyers. 'We weren't gonna make the movie without the right kid.'

After wading through a production line of mediocre performances, the producers stumbled upon Lindsay's tape. 'She was girl 412,' recalls Nancy proudly. 'She'd been on a soap but I knew nothing else about her.' Something instantly caught the team's attention. 'I saw Lindsay's tape, and I heard the lines for the first time,' said Nancy. 'She did quirky things, made faces. She's animated... brilliant, it turns out.'

Nancy already knew the type of actress she was looking for and – fingers crossed – she'd found her. 'I love Diane Keaton; I've done three movies with her and the kinds of things I write she does real well. She makes things fresh and spontaneous and, for a filmmaker, that's exciting. I didn't want a kid I would programme. I was looking for a young Diane.'

Lindsay was one of five actresses invited to screen test. Thrilled at the opportunity, she travelled to LA with her family in tow. She would spend a week working with acting coaches to learn an English accent for the part and ensure she gave her best performance. Each candidate wore the same outfit and had to film a screen test with Dennis Quaid.

Lindsay remembers her audition clearly. 'I had to get choked up and cry a little bit,' she recalls. 'But I was so nervous because there were like 50 million people there and I was working with a famous actor. Everyone made me feel comfortable with it because everyone on the set was really fun.'

As it turned out, Lindsay had nothing to worry about. Her performance had more than sufficiently impressed the directors. 'Lindsay was the first one up,' says director Charles Shyer. 'I leaned over to Nancy [Meyer] and said, "This one is going to be hard to beat." She's just a winner. The minute the cameras rolled, something happened with Lindsay. It was just that magical "it" you can't describe.'

Nancy was now confident her initial instincts had been correct – she'd found the star she was so desperately seeking. 'Lindsay was extremely spunky and enthusiastic,' says Nancy. 'She was like a little Diane Keaton – gifted as a comedian but who doesn't know it.'

Having to give fair consideration to the other candidates involved, the production team were careful not to give too much away. Lindsay had no idea the role was already hers for the taking.

Straight after the audition, Dina took her for a milkshake to celebrate. Ever the perfectionist, Lindsay couldn't help but analyse her performance in minute detail, picking fault where none actually existed. But, like any young kid, she was easily distracted. No sooner had Dina presented Lindsay with her favourite McDonald's Happy Meal than all thoughts of rolling cameras and bright studio lights evaporated from her mind. For now, she had far greater concerns. 'Eugh, I hate gherkins!' she squealed.

The following morning, Lindsay received a phone call in her hotel room. She'd been awake half the night wondering whether she'd be lucky on this occasion. Due to work commitments in New York, Dina had flown home the previous evening, and Michael was left taking care of Lindsay in LA. Keen not to raise her hopes unnecessarily, Dina and Michael had avoided discussing the audition with their daughter. Deep down, both parents knew their daughter was more than capable of handling the role, but logic never really applied in the world of showbusiness. Who could tell what the directors were really after? One of the girls auditioning had been English, making her ideally suited to the part. Dina knew Lindsay could handle disappointment and rejection, but it never grew any easier.

Lindsay picked up the receiver apprehensively and closed her eyes. Seconds later, a smile crept across her lips. Unable to contain her excitement any longer, she hung up and let out a scream. The part was hers. 'I started screaming and jumping on the bed and my dad started crying,' she recalls. 'Two seconds later, I called my mom and she started crying, and my brothers and sister, too. I found out in a really cool way. It was the first movie I was ever up for and I couldn't believe I got it. I would go to bed and pray that I could be in a movie. One in a million chance, y'know?'

Landing a role in a major feature film had a dramatic impact not only on Lindsay's life but also on her entire family. At the time, the acting protégé was only 11 years old and still required parental supervision. Lindsay's family chose to accompany her on set wherever possible. While some scenes were filmed in a studio, others were shot on location in California's Napa Valley and London.

Keen to follow in their sister's footsteps, most of the Lohan clan appeared in front of the camera. Lindsay's brother Michael played a lost boy at camp who finds himself in a fencing competition with Hallie and Annie.

Playing identical twins proved to be a real challenge for Lindsay; both characters had completely different personalities and accents. 'I would just keep in mind that Hallie was more spunky and that Annie was the reserved one,' says Lindsay.

During scenes where Hallie and Annie were together, Lindsay had to play each sister in separate takes with a stand-in actress, recalling every little detail of their interchange. 'It was an amazing feat,' says Nancy Meyers.

Even Lindsay's friends were confused by her dual identity when the film finally came out. 'They thought, "Who's that other girl that looks just like Lindsay?" And I said, "That girl is me!"' she laughs. 'When I saw the movie, though, I noticed first about how different we were dressed but also how one girl had more freckles than the other. It was crazy how they did it.'

During one particular scene, the script required Lindsay's character Annie to go skinny-dipping after losing a game of poker at summer camp. She refers to it as one of the hardest moments on set. 'I had to be in a lake late at night, and I had to stay in there for like two hours. It was so-o-o cold,' she shivers. 'They put this heating machine in the lake, but it didn't do much good.'

Despite being a novice to the film industry, Lindsay gave a remarkable performance, going on to win a Young Artist Award for her role. Even when Lindsay made her first mistake, the crew were quick to offer encouragement. 'They all applauded and said, "Welcome to the movie business,"' she says.

On set, her professionalism and good manners earned the respect of her co-stars. Natasha Richardson and Dennis Quaid both took the young actress under their wing, giving her invaluable guidance and career advice. Dennis became so fond of the 'little pro' he even presented her with a Prada knapsack. 'She knows what she's doing,' he said. 'She has a really good work ethic. But she's still a little girl, which is a good thing.'

Even when the cameras had finished rolling, Lindsay was keen to entertain her newfound friends. Nancy Meyers recalls that the excitable young girl would often come into her own trailer. 'She and my daughter would play really loud music and dance like crazy.' Her natural talent quickly registered with the director. 'Comedy is something you can't teach or explain,' says Nancy. 'Lindsay just gets it. She's wise beyond her years. She's such a naturally gifted actress that even the demanding stuff was fun for her.'

In her down-time, Lindsay was busy exploring the more glamorous trappings of a Hollywood lifestyle. The whole experience of living in a new city proved to be very exciting, but a little overwhelming at times. Now she was a bona fide movie star, Lindsay wanted to make sure she looked the part. After hitting the boutiques in LA, she waltzed on set one day with a Versace coat and a Kate Spade bag. Although she was given a weekly allowance, she had persuaded Dina to splash out on designer goods. It was the beginning of a love affair with shopping that would become an integral part of her nature.

Aside from her increasingly adult attire, Lindsay was still a little girl who enjoyed playing with friends. She would often watch videos and sunbathe with her stand-in actress. One weekend, some friends from New York travelled down to LA for a visit. 'We made a big mess in the hotel room,' smiles Lindsay. 'We'd sprayed my brother with shaving cream for a joke.' But one morning, while her parents were sleeping, he took revenge. 'He took whipped cream, coffee and miles of sugar and threw it on me!' she laughs.

While for the most part Lindsay enjoyed her new career as a film actress, the physical demands of making a movie left her drained and exhausted. 'That movie took seven months, three weeks and two days to film,' she recalls with painstaking precision. 'It was a lot at once and I was really young. It was just very overwhelming. All my friends were still in school and I missed them.'

It had been eight months since Lindsay was last in full-time education. When she returned home, many of her classmates were puzzled as to where she had been. Worried about the reaction she might receive, she told them her family had simply been on a long vacation. But when *The Parent Trap* finally came out, it was a huge success, grossing $66 million at the US box office. Lindsay was interviewed on talk shows like *Good Morning America* and *The Rosie O'Donnell Show* and quickly became a household name. 'My friends were like, "Um... Lindsay? That's you in *Parent Trap*?" And I said, "Oh yeah, I also did this movie while we were gone."'

While filming *The Parent Trap*, Lindsay also completed a modelling job for Abercrombie & Fitch. The campaign launch happened to coincide with her film release, making the once anonymous model an overnight celebrity. Her photograph appeared on giant store posters and shopping bags. 'I went to the mall with my friends right after the film came out,' she says. 'When we walked into Abercrombie, everyone's attention doubled and everybody was just coming up to me.'

Initially, Lindsay found fame difficult to handle. This was new and uncharted territory. Although she'd been warned about what might happen and had been a fan of film stars herself, she wasn't prepared for the impact she would have on an audience. 'People were telling me that I wouldn't be able to go out as much for a little bit, because it would be overwhelming. But I was 13 years old, I wanted to go to the mall with my friends. There were posters of the movie up all over. Girls my age and younger were coming up to me to get an autograph, as well as parents asking for their kids. I didn't know what to do. When I went home, I started thinking of different signatures,' she recalls.

Afraid she'd be labelled a show-off, Lindsay preferred to remain inconspicuous. Her friends were often shocked to see people come up and ask for an autograph, but Lindsay was grateful for the attention.

'It's really a good thing to know you mean that much to people.'

Lindsay Lohan's star was in the ascendance. Disney were overjoyed with their new golden girl and had snapped her up for a three-picture deal. With Lindsay firmly embedded in the public consciousness, now would be the ideal time to seize new opportunities and capitalise on her success. But, to everyone's amazement, Lindsay did the exact opposite. Taking one of the biggest risks in her career, she chose to shelve the filmmaking and return to school. Filming *The Parent Trap* had been a fantastic experience, but she was acutely aware that life at home was going on without her. She was tired and missed playing football and attending cheerleading practice like other normal teenagers. She was also keen to follow in the footsteps of her idol Jodie Foster who 'also knew reality and went to school'.

Despite her own ambitions for Lindsay's success, Dina was eager to apply the brakes; she had seen too many precocious starlets swallowed up by the industry. The last thing she wanted her daughter to develop was an unbearable ego. If Lindsay was going to become a truly great actress, it was important for her to experience a dose of normal everyday life. 'She told me, "I know you want to do this and that's great and I'll support you, but I want you to go to school now and I want you to be with your friends and have a normal life,'" recalls Lindsay with gratitude. 'She was right. I think that normality keeps you grounded. My mother knew the dangers because she was dancing and acting at a young age as well.'

Looking back, Dina realises her decision could have backfired. 'It was a gamble for me as a mom,' she admits. 'Because I didn't want her to grow up hating me. But, if she'd stayed in Hollywood, she'd be a nightmare by now. Kids need boundaries.'

Desperate to keep their new star in the limelight, Disney offered Lindsay the role of Penny in *Inspector Gadget*, alongside Matthew Broderick. Although tempted, she remained steadfastly committed to her plans and turned down the part. Michelle Trachtenberg, who would later play Dawn in *Buffy the Vampire Slayer*, later stepped into the role.

In retrospect, Lindsay believes wholeheartedly that she made the right decision. 'I see a lot of girls that are my age who are very caught up in the business. They walk around like they're hot. People think that, because you have everyone willing to do everything for you. If you're a kid and you have that, that's scary.'

Even today, Lindsay admits she is shocked to see young Hollywood stars flouncing around film studios with an assistant in tow. 'Now when kids go into the business young, their parents get so involved – it's like the scariest thing I've ever seen. I've seen little kids that have assistants. That's just weird. But I would say to anyone – be true to yourself. Be with your friends and your family first.'

Unfortunately, not everyone in the Lohan family was quite so level-headed. While Lindsay's success had provided a momentary distraction from family woes, not long after Lindsay had wrapped on *The Parent Trap*, she came home to find her father was 'away' yet again. Found guilty of stock fraud, he'd been sent to prison for four years. At first, Dina refused to tell her children the truth, for fear the reality would be too upsetting. Instead, she told them their father was extremely busy working away on a job. 'I finally figured it out,' Lindsay would later confess. 'I was like, "Mom, I'm not an idiot."'

Despite the pain Michael had caused his family, Lindsay continued to defend her father. 'Somebody screwed him over,' she would later argue, casually dismissing his criminal conviction. 'This kind of thing has happened to so many people I know it's almost, like, normal.'

To some extent, she may have been right. Michael Lohan operated in a business world riddled with snakes, dishing out handshakes with one hand, while using the other to stab you in the back. Desperate to maintain the lavish lifestyle his family currently enjoyed, Michael would find himself involved in a number of schemes with any profits quickly reinvested.

Lindsay was quickly learning that, wherever money is involved, few people could be trusted.

But Lindsay remained steadfast; even though her father had allegedly broken the law, she would stand by him. Only recently has she stopped excusing his wayward behaviour on every occasion. 'When my dad would do things, it used to really hurt me. At the same time, he's the best dad. He's the most loving, kind person you'd ever meet. My parents are working some things out right now.'

Often ashamed of his actions in more contemplative moments, Michael would praise his daughter for her strength. 'Lindsay is such a tough kid. She bore so much. My children are angels.'

It didn't take long for news of Michael's arrest to spread throughout the neighbourhood. Just as Lindsay had become an overnight local celebrity, Michael shot to notoriety for all the wrong reasons. Constant classroom taunts left Lindsay feeling miserable. Her family life had become too exposed and Dina decided it was time to move on. Lindsay swapped her swanky school on the North Shore for a more working-class community on the South Shore. Her life as a normal teenager wasn't exactly going to plan.

3

SCHOOL DAZE

Although Lindsay encountered a few teething problems, she quickly settled into her new school, Sanford H Calhoun High. Excelling in maths and science, she matured into an A-grade student. Although some people would treat her differently because of her fame, Lindsay made an effort to get along with everyone. 'If you're an actress, people assume that you think you're better than everyone else. I wanted to make sure that people had no reason to think that about me.'

Well versed in the art of playground politics, Lindsay quickly aligned herself with every social group going. Describing herself as 'a floater', she was accepted by everyone. 'There would be girls I knew who were only in one clique, and their friends wouldn't be in school that day so they'd have no one to talk to. That scared me, so that's why I wanted to try and get along with everyone.' Taking care to abide by certain codes of conduct, she quickly learned that different groups stuck to certain hangouts around the school. Preferring to stand on the sidelines, Lindsay tried to avoid any major arguments. 'If someone is going to say something to me, I just let it go. That freaks people out sometimes. When you say something back to someone who's speaking badly of you, that just drags the whole thing out. [I'd rather] kill them with kindness.'

As is the case with most teenage girls, boys were often at the centre of feuds between Lindsay and her friends. 'Girls love drama! It gives them something to do. But, when you get older, it's kind of a hassle.'

But, while Lindsay vied for male attention with her own peers, a completely unexpected threat emerged – her own mother. Dina had always been considered good-looking in her youth and even now it was difficult to imagine she was hitting 40. Slim, blonde and always decked out in the latest fashions, she was what guys would call a 'yummy mummy'. 'It was hard because she'd come up to school to get me and the guys would give her a standing ovation in the cafeteria. I was like, "Mom, don't pick me up. I'll walk to you. You don't have to come in." So many guys were hitting on my mom. They were like, "God, why can't you look like your mom?" I was like, "I'm sorry!"'

Although Lindsay would grow up to be a sex symbol with a substantial male following, she was always self-conscious about her looks. School quickly became a battleground for fashion-savvy girls sporting the latest designer labels. Image often equated with acceptance, and choosing the right outfit became a daily trauma. 'A lot of the girls want to be cool and wear the same sweat pants outfits like Juicy Couture,' she says looking back. 'You're learning to find yourself and that process in difficult. Everyone tends to be very critical and you always want to be popular. There's a lot to worry about.'

Born with flowing red hair and a crop of freckles, Lindsay would immediately stand out from the crowd. But, although her individual looks had secured the pretty young girl a modelling contract, she felt constantly uncomfortable with her appearance and desperately wanted to look like everyone else. On one occasion, Lindsay became obsessed with the idea of having a layered haircut similar to the one made famous by Jennifer Aniston on *Friends*.

Despite her insistence, Dina refused to let Lindsay cut her long her. But the stubborn teenager was adamant; she'd made up her mind and no one could stop her. One afternoon during an art lesson, Lindsay snuck to the back of her classroom and chopped off her red locks. She arrived home looking a shambles and Dina had no choice but to rush her straight to the hair salon for a rescue operation. A layered cut turned out to be the only solution available. Lindsay was triumphant – she had got exactly what she wanted. Manipulating a situation to her advantage was a skill the astute young woman would employ increasingly in her career.

'I used to hate my red hair,' she admits. 'I wanted it to be blonde so bad because my mom had blonde hair.' Lindsay also felt a lot of pressure to wear make-up, mainly to cover up her freckles. During the summer, she would avoid the sun for fear it would cause an even greater break-out. While bathing by the pool, she would longingly admire her bronzed friends with apparently perfect skin. 'My friends have that skin, that flawless, no-freckles skin. Mine is just annoying to me.' Over time, Lindsay came to accept her freckles as a unique trademark and a feature to be cherished rather than loathed. 'I just think, "Suck it up and have fun." Who wants to sit around thinking about what they don't like about their looks?'

Settling into life as a normal teenager wasn't quite the cruise Lindsay had imagined. Having enjoyed her taste of Hollywood fame, she was soon eager to get back in front of the camera after only a year away. She missed the buzz and excitement of being on set. While filming *The Parent Trap*, she'd travelled extensively; now she rarely left Long

Island. She also found it hard watching other young stars break the big time. Watching her contemporaries on TV interviews, she felt a pang of jealousy. There was also a nagging concern that, if Lindsay didn't move quickly, she'd be missing out. 'I started seeing other girls working more,' she says. 'I was bored of just going to school and I remembered what it was like working on movies. I missed having posters of me everywhere.' Satisfied that Lindsay had enjoyed a sufficient taste of real teenage life, Dina agreed it was time to move forward with her career.

Disney were quick to offer Lindsay a TV-movie role without asking her to audition. Executives had been patiently waiting for the new talent to make her return. The schedule was much shorter than that of a feature film, allowing Lindsay to fit in her schooling. It seemed to be the perfect compromise. Lindsay flew to Vancouver to film *Life-Size* alongside supermodel Tyra Banks, The role itself proved challenging. Lindsay played a young girl, Casey, grieving over the death of her mother. 'It's a really hard thing to lose your mother, and I haven't experienced that, thank God,' she said at the time. 'But that was one of the many things I had to realise when I was getting to know my character. I had to put all those thoughts in my head and try to become the character I was playing so I could make it as real as possible.'

While filming, Lindsay also developed a friendship with Tyra Banks and even attended her birthday party. She would return home from set gushing to Dina about how 'nice' and 'normal' her new mentor had been. 'It's not every day you get to work with a supermodel!' she jokes. But, if Lindsay had felt insecure about her looks before, standing next to a towering catwalk queen was a true test of confidence. 'Tyra was so tall. She always wore sneakers when we were shooting. But when she wasn't in sneakers, I was like, "You can't stand next to me."'

Around the same time, 13-year-old Lindsay shot a pilot for a TV adaptation of Bette Midler's life and career, in which she was cast as Bette's daughter Rose. But, after only one episode, the production team moved the show to LA. Once again, Lindsay was forced to choose between her professional and personal life. She thought long and hard about joining them, but the timing wasn't right. She wasn't ready to sacrifice her friends and family just yet. As it turned out, the show was cancelled after just one month and, by that time, Lindsay was already busy with her next role as amateur sleuth Lexy Gold in the Disney TV movie *Get a Clue*.

As her career gradually picked up again, Lindsay found it increasingly difficult to balance her schoolwork with the demands of TV schedules. Her classroom peers were also starting to treat Lindsay differently, with her success becoming a focus for jealousy. While teachers happily consented to her frequent absences, other pupils accused her of receiving special treatment. Several agreed that she needed to be taught a lesson. Quite maliciously, they started excluding her from activities.

One incident sticks out clearly in Lindsay's mind. Most of Lindsay's class had been invited to a house party and, for once, the heavily booked-up actress was in town. It had been ages since Lindsay had relaxed with friends, and she was looking forward to an opportunity to hang out. Besides, plenty of hot boys would be at the party, so there would definitely be lots of gossip to share on Monday morning. But not everyone was so enthusiastic about Lindsay's invite. Suspicious of her Hollywood profile, one group of girls assumed she was a stuck-up bitch. They also feared most boys at the party would make an instant beeline for the celebrity redhead. In an attempt to isolate her from the gathering, they threatened to beat Lindsay up. The sensitive young star was shocked and hurt by their open hostility, but she wasn't wholly surprised. On Dina's advice, she attempted to befriend the girls and prove them wrong. As her mother pointed out, their physical threats were simply a response to the emotional threats Lindsay posed. If she could convince her peers she was just a normal teen and allay their insecurities, perhaps they might finally accept her.

After a great deal of hard work and persuasion, Lindsay eventually won the girls over. Handling the situation with maturity, she understood why girls automatically felt threatened by an actress in their midst. 'Girls can get pretty catty. They never really got to know me because I was never really there.' Offering advice to young girls who might find themselves in a similar situation, she added, 'I think it's important in high school to be yourself and surround yourself with friends that you can trust.'

Although Lindsay had worked hard to win friends at school, watching her back every day had become too much like hard work. She was exhausted by the constant need to justify herself to every new person. However much she might try to disguise the fact, Lindsay Lohan was no normal average American teen. She'd grown up surrounded by adults and felt far more at home on a film set than in a playground. Anyhow, forces were pulling this talented young lady in a different direction. By eleventh grade, Lindsay's schooldays were drawing to a close. Dina agreed to her request for home schooling and enrolled Lindsay with the Laurel Springs School, famed for tutoring young celebrities. Several of Lindsay's young actor friends were landing high-profile roles and she could no longer conceal her desire to take up acting full-time. Dina recalls, 'She'd see some of her friends surpassing her and she's like, "I have to do this."'

Once again, the aspiring actress had firmly made up her mind – she wanted to star in another movie. On this occasion, no one would dare stand in her way.

4

TEEN FREAK

Lindsay had often cited Oscar-winning actress Jodie Foster as one of her acting idols. When an audition came up for a remake of the 1976 Disney classic *Freaky Friday*, the film that originally propelled Foster to fame, the now 15-year-old Lindsay knew it would be the perfect reintroduction to the movie business.

The storyline revolved around a girl called Anna who unwillingly switches bodies with her mother. A rebellious teen who torments her younger brother and plays in a rock band with two friends, Anna shares a poor relationship with her mum, a widowed psychotherapist who is about to remarry. But, thanks to a mysterious Chinese spell, the pair awake on the day of the wedding rehearsal to find themselves literally in each other's shoes. As the day unfolds, they end up in a series of comedy scrapes and eventually find common ground through their shared experiences.

Lindsay fell instantly in love with the script. Although it would be her second Disney remake, she dismissed any suggestion that she'd been typecast. 'People were like, "Oh, she's going to do all the remakes now." If you do it the right way, then there's nothing wrong with that.' Commenting on the challenge of playing a character three times her age, she said, 'When you play certain characters, people my age have a tendency to be typecast, so it's great to find a film where I can play something that's completely different from everyone my age.'

Even before she'd secured the part, Lindsay developed a feel for her character. Originally, the part of Anna was written as a Goth, but Lindsay disagreed with the description. 'No one could relate to the character when she was really Goth,' she complained. 'There was nothing there.'

Lindsay watched the original version of *Freaky Friday*, but decided she wanted to bring something new to the film. Besides, there was no point in trying to imitate Jodie Foster. She'd already done a fantastic job. 'I didn't want to try to be like Jodie Foster and do a terrible job and be really embarrassed,' said Lindsay wisely. Convinced her interpretation of the character was far better than the director's, she restructured the part for her audition. 'I wore a collared turquoise Abercrombie & Fitch shirt and khaki pants, swear to God, with a white headband. And my hair was really straight and pretty and red and blonde. My agent calls and was like, "What are you doing?"'

But Lindsay's risk paid off. The studio were suitably impressed by her adaptation and rewrote the part completely. 'We did a nationwide search, every major city in the country, and saw thousands of girls and tested a dozen of them,' said writer-director Mark Waters. 'When I tested Lindsay, the way she took direction, I felt I was with an Olympic athlete. It was like the triple jump. She had that talent level to work with me at that ease and also that fiery energy, which I wanted for Anna. After I saw Lindsay, there was no number two. I was scared.'

Absent from the film scene for so long, Lindsay was eager to tackle her new role. But several casting problems delayed filming. Annette Bening, who won a Golden Globe for her role in *American Beauty*, was originally cast as Anna's mother but dropped out at the last minute. Singer and TV celebrity Kelly Osbourne also turned down her part as Anna's best friend, after her mother Sharon was diagnosed with colon cancer. Initially, Lindsay was disappointed, as she'd relished the opportunity of working with both stars. But, ultimately, a change in personnel turned out to be a blessing in disguise.

Jamie Lee Curtis stepped in to take over the role of Anna's mother. Lindsay was already familiar with her films. 'I'd seen all her *Halloween* stuff. They were so scary but I forced myself to see them with my brother and his friend, and I loved them.'

Lindsay already regarded her co-star as a brilliant actress. 'She just has this thing about her when she's on screen, you just can't stop looking.' Jamie quickly developed a bond with Lindsay and became a mentor to the ambitious star. Lindsay identified several similarities between herself and the seasoned veteran; both women were outgoing, down-to-earth and, most importantly, they enjoyed having a laugh. 'She's a really good person and really confident, but at the same time really cool,' enthused Lindsay. 'It's like the greatest combination, and she's everything that I want to be when I'm her age. She is so comfortable with herself, and it's so great to see that.'

In return, Jamie lavished compliments on her talented co-star. She was impressed with the way Lindsay handled her character and with her impeccable sense of comic timing. 'This doesn't happen a lot,' she told Lindsay. 'If it does, it's alchemy.'

Mimicking each other's characters on screen tested the abilities of both actresses. They would carefully study tapes of each other's performance to make the portrayal realistic. 'I think that was a great idea on Mark Waters's part. We sat in a room, Jamie and I, and she read the whole script as she would have read it, as if there was no changing. It sort of helped us figure out little gestures that Jamie would do in a scene and it would help me become more like her character,' explained Lindsay. She also sought valuable guidance on playing an adult from her own mother. 'My mom stands a certain way and she has really good posture. So I took that from her. Whenever I slouch, she goes over and she puts my back up straight. But my mom is really cool and Jamie's character in the film is very square. I think my mom is more like Jamie in real life.'

On reflection, Lindsay believes her role in *Freaky Friday* gave her a greater insight into the responsibilities her own mum has to bear. Up until now, she'd never really taken the time to stop and appreciate the sacrifices Dina had made for her career. Being a mother, manager and chauffeur was a near-impossible feat. Lindsay recognised that her mother was not only loving, but also extremely determined. It was a quality they both shared. 'I think I am my mom,' Lindsay laughs. 'She even looks like me – but with blonder hair. But I don't think I could be her for the day. I never really took the time to realise how much she does – from getting us all to school and running around town. This is a great movie for mothers and daughters to see together. Girls my age hide things from their parents, and I think it's important to speak to your parents and let them know what's going on. It's like you always want what you can't have, and, with certain teen girls, if their parents are saying they can't do certain things, they're going to want to do them even more.'

Just as Lindsay had impressed the film crew on *The Parent Trap*, she quickly earned respect from *Freaky Friday* director Mark Waters, who described her as a real pro. 'Lindsay Lohan is nothing like the character of Anna, who's this bad-attitude, punk-rocking, tough girl – almost a tomboy. That's not who Lindsay is, and yet she's pulled that off brilliantly.'

But it was the massive disparity between Anna's personality and her own that Lindsay found most appealing. 'Anna kind of keeps everything inside, rather than saying how she feels.'

In the three years since her last big-screen appearance, Lindsay had grown up a great deal. No longer a child, greater expectations were placed on her as a young woman. While teenagers her age were experiencing their first bouts of young love, it was inevitable Lindsay would soon have to do the same on camera. Her first on-screen kiss was with *Dawson's Creek* and *One Tree Hill* pin-up Chad Michael Murray. Although Lindsay was the envy of her friends, she was dreading the scenes. 'I talked to Chad before and I was like, "Listen… I'm really nervous. You might not be nervous because you've done it before, but I'm really nervous. Just know that."'

The scene took two days to shoot and Lindsay admits that, on the whole, it wasn't an entirely unpleasant experience. 'He's really good-looking. I know a lot of girls who are obsessed with Chad, so that was a huge plus for me. And he's really sweet, too.'

Thankfully, Lindsay's first on-screen kiss proved to be a lot less stressful than her first real-life experience. She recalls it took place at a friend's house during eighth grade. 'It was with someone that I really liked and I guess that's all that matters.' Suffering an uncharacteristic loss of confidence, she nervously wondered who would make the first move. 'Is he going to do it? Am I? When do I stop? It's awkward!' she would later confess.

Already, *Freaky Friday* was shaping up to be an educational experience. Lindsay ventured into even more new territory when she recorded a song for the soundtrack and performed on film. Originally, Kelly Osbourne had been pencilled in to sing 'Ultimate', but her departure left the door wide open for Lindsay. She informed Mark Waters of her lifelong ambition to sing and, once again, her wish was granted. Although Lindsay was better known as an actress, she'd been singing and dancing for as long as she'd been in the movies. But it would be difficult to emerge as a singer right away, because so many other young stars were doing exactly the same thing. 'It's hard right now because there are a lot of young girls coming out. There's Hilary [Duff] and Britney... I don't want to just be one in the pack. I want to separate myself.'

Dina was acutely aware that carving out a successful career was often down to considered timing. To unleash 'Lindsay the pop star' on an audience only recently acquainted with her acting talents would be overkill. Lindsay agreed. 'I'm kind of just meeting with people and feeling it out. I'm not gonna jump into anything, because I'm busy working with other stuff. I don't want to jump into it. I think the music industry is all about timing. I want to wait until I'm older, so, if I do want to act a certain way or sing certain lyrics and stuff, it's age appropriate.' Recording a song for the soundtrack was at least a tentative step in the right direction.

Lindsay took up guitar lessons for her scenes with the band, and confessed she'd always wanted an excuse to learn. 'Guitar is always something that I've been interested in, so, when I had the chance to learn, I figured, why not take it?' Admittedly, she didn't play on the soundtrack itself, but she was determined to keep up her new hobby. 'When I have time, I'm gonna take lessons and stuff,' she promised at the time.

Lindsay was already spending a great deal of her spare time writing lyrics. 'It's really easy for me to sit down and, once I learn to play guitar, it's only going to benefit me in terms of writing.'

Looking for an artist with whom her audience would immediately identify, Lindsay based her character in *Freaky Friday* on pop-punk singer Avril Lavigne. 'Whenever I was playing the guitar, that's who I tried to think of, just 'cause she has a coolness about her that was perfect for Anna. Girls my age can relate because Avril is someone everyone knows.' The film soundtrack, boosted by Lindsay's song, even entered the Billboard Top 20.

The American public wholeheartedly warmed to Lindsay's performance. Following in Jodie Foster's footsteps was a tricky task, but Lindsay adapted the character sufficiently and made it her own. 'Jodie Foster's character was more of a tomboy and my character's more of a punk rocker. It's modernised, which is necessary for the audience to like it. Everything is taken up a notch.' When Lindsay later heard that Jodie had watched her new version and given her approval, she was over the moon.

Jamie and Lindsay both received favourable reviews from critics. Neither of them had expected such an overwhelming response. 'The whole time we were filming, we kept saying we were going to suck,' said Lindsay. When the film emerged to be a surprise hit, Jamie printed two T-shirts with the slogan 'We didn't suck' and gave one to Lindsay as a present.

The film's success also reflected in financial figures, pulling in over $100 million at the North American box office. Disney Studios chairman Dick Cook took the opportunity to thank Lindsay for her hard work. He invited the bubbly teen into his office and presented her with an envelope. 'We have this little present for you,' he said.

Intrigued by what it might be, Lindsay desperately tried to peer through the paper. She finally ripped it open to find a bonus cheque for £1 million inside. 'That's a lot of money!' she gasped. 'My parents' friends don't even have that much money, and they're 40 or 50 years old.'

Disney clearly realised they'd nurtured a lucrative talent. No longer a promising child star, Lindsay Lohan was now a formidable force in the teen market. Financially, she could start calling the shots.

5
THE RIVALS

W hen *Freaky Friday* hit cinema screens in 2003, Lindsay Lohan was once again hot property in the press. But, this time, demands made on the teenage actress were a little different. After *The Parent Trap*, she appeared in several magazines for young girls. Now three years on, the teen press had developed an interest in the charismatic redhead and soon the dreaded tabloids would follow suit. While Lindsay had proved herself to be a valuable commodity on screen, she was equally adept at shifting units on the magazine shelves.

Just as Lindsay had taken control of her character's look in *Freaky Friday*, she was keen to be involved in the way her own image was portrayed. She would arrive at shoots with pages ripped from fashion magazines. 'I tore pages out of this month's *Elle*,' she told one photographer, referring them to a feature with Kirsten Dunst. 'I love her make-up in this. It looks so pretty. Let's do that.' Carefully scrutinising items on the stylist's fashion rail, she'd pick out designer garments from Rock & Republic, Citizens of Humanity and Chloe. 'I always go for the pink. I love pink!' she told one journalist, producing a pink Baby Phat mobile phone from her handbag in evidence. Clearly, Lindsay had been putting her new spending power to good use.

In the spring of 2003, Lindsay received a phone call from prestigious lifestyle magazine *Vanity Fair* inviting her to appear on the cover of an edition devoted entirely to young rising talent. Her inclusion in a line-up alongside Mary-Kate and Ashley Olsen, Mandy Moore and Hilary Duff was proof that Lindsay had been accepted into the exclusive superstar teen league. She was incredibly flattered and agreed to take part. Dina was thrilled, aware this would be an ideal opportunity to boost her daughter's profile internationally. Lindsay, meanwhile, couldn't wait to rifle through the wealth of lavish outfits that would certainly be on offer. There appeared to be only one concern for her and that was Hilary Duff.

Given that Lindsay and Hilary were both successful Disney teen queens, it seemed inevitable gossips would pit them against each other in the press. While Lindsay was still honing her craft on *Freaky Friday*,

Hilary had shot to prominence in the Disney sitcom *Lizzie McGuire* and starred in an eponymous film adaptation. She'd also released an album, *Metamorphosis*, and Lindsay had never disguised her own passion for singing. When Lindsay arrived on the scene, she posed an obvious threat to Hilary's comfortable position atop the teen ladder. Initially, both girls joked about their friendly rivalry and tried desperately hard to forge their own career paths. Hilary even described the pair as 'phone pals'. 'We used to speak on the phone while I was filming *Lizzie McGuire* and she was doing a Disney Channel movie,' she said.

But Hollywood is a small world and soon both actresses were competing for the same film roles. 'When you're acting and you're around girls your age, everyone wants to be like each other,' shrugged Lindsay. 'To be in a position where you're always going to be compared to other girls near your age who are great actresses and not get horribly insecure about it or obsess about it is hard. There's always going to be somebody else auditioning for the same role. There's always going to be another girl who's doing the same thing as you. And if you're always going to be competitive about who's getting which roles, you're never going to be satisfied or have fun and appreciate the fact that you're doing these movies.'

But, while Lindsay and Hilary could both cope

with healthy competition in their professional careers, rivalry in their personal lives was a different matter. When they eventually fell out, it was predictably over a love interest. During the filming of *Freaky Friday* in 2002, Lindsay struck up a relationship with pop star Aaron Carter, the younger brother of Backstreet Boys singer Nick. The couple attended several public events together and Aaron was even photographed with Lindsay slicing a birthday cake on her sweet sixteenth. But then Lindsay discovered Aaron was dating Hilary! The press quickly capitalised on the story and it made headline news. Although Lindsay had bickered with friends over boys at school, having her private life on show for public viewing was a completely different matter. The whole episode made her feel very uncomfortable.

A young and naive celebrity new to the press game, Lindsay fell into the tabloid trap of reacting to stories. In the past, she'd proudly proclaimed her honesty to be one of her best personality traits, but on this occasion it only landed her in further trouble. She told a national newspaper that someone had left a message on her answerphone saying she was 'fat and needed to do Pilates'. Gossip columnists instantly pounced on the story, speculating further to fuel the rivalry.

A few weeks later, rotten eggs were thrown at Hilary's Range Rover. Lindsay denied involvement explaining that she was out of town on a promotional commitment at the time. In an attempt to set the record straight and put an end to the dispute, Lindsay told US daily morning TV show *Good Morning America*, 'My thing with Hilary is a high-school thing. It's the reason why I wanted to finish school early. When you are working, the last thing you want to read is someone doesn't like you. Let it go.'

The story was already well documented by the time Lindsay and Hilary were both invited to pose for *Vanity Fair*. The other actresses attending were prepared for a fiery exchange between the two rivals. On the morning of the shoot, Lindsay could hardly eat her breakfast. Any excitement about taking part was marred by concern that a scene might erupt between herself and Hilary. Dina advised her daughter to act like an adult and rise above the childish gossip. Lindsay agreed. Taking a deep breath, she made her grand entrance.

She was secretly relieved to discover that Hilary was running late. At least she'd have time to familiarise herself with the set-up, meet a few of the other stars and settle her nerves. One person she really hit it off with was Mary-Kate Olsen. The pair had plenty of mutual friends in LA. They exchanged numbers and agreed to keep in touch. Journalists from the magazine came over to introduce themselves and made Lindsay feel instantly at ease.

In one corner, a huge table had been laid with a

banquet of food – bowls of pasta, salad, chips, sweets... Lindsay couldn't believe her eyes. Oddly, none of the other girls had even made moves to take any. Lindsay shrugged – she wasn't about to let good food go to waste. In a hurry that morning, she'd forgotten to eat breakfast. As she tucked into a bowl of pasta, several of the girls glanced over. Lindsay suddenly felt uncomfortable and wondered if there was something ridiculous stuck to her hair. Had she forgotten to cut the price label from her new jumper? Did she have toothpaste smeared all over her face? After a few minutes, it dawned on her – the girls weren't staring at Lindsay, they were salivating over the food. Judging by most of their minuscule waist sizes, it had been a long time since any of them had enjoyed a proper dinner. Dina had always been strict with Lindsay and forced her to eat properly. She never had less than her three meals a day.

As Lindsay defiantly spooned in her last mouthful of pasta, she was distracted by a commotion outside in the hallway. On walking over to ascertain the source of so much noise, she discovered that Hilary Duff had arrived. But she wasn't alone. Lindsay's face dropped, and she felt her stomach sink like a lead balloon. Hilary had invited Aaron!

Suddenly, all eyes were on Lindsay. She felt her face burn red with embarrassment. Remembering her mother's words, she tried to pull herself together and get on with the shoot. After all, she was a professional. But, as the day wore on, it became increasingly hard to concentrate. Feeling uncomfortable and unable to focus on the shoot, Lindsay finally gave in and asked representatives from *Vanity Fair* to evict her love interest. Aware of the much-publicised love triangle, they sympathetically agreed. Hilary, however, was incensed and protested. Aaron was her boyfriend and she saw no reason why he should be forced to leave, eventually breaking down in floods of tears.

After that day, relations between Lindsay and Hilary deteriorated even further. To make matters worse, Aaron waded in to offer his version of events. His comments to the press were extremely upsetting to Lindsay. He claimed she had stirred up animosity unnecessarily and insisted he was with Hilary first. 'Lindsay is a troublemaker!' he snarled years later. 'She always has been, and that's coming from knowing her for five years. When I broke up with her in 2002, I said, "Goodbye! I don't want any more of you!" She was really, really possessive. My brother Nick told me to stay away from her.'

Since then, Lindsay and Aaron have had very little contact, although in a recent interview Aaron claimed his brother had bumped into Lindsay in an LA club. 'She was really, really rude to him for no reason. Nick said to her, "I know why you're being mean. It's because of my brother!"'

As is the case with most love triangles, no one involved is ever entirely blameless. In years to come, Lindsay and Hilary would both wonder why they'd wasted so much energy worrying about a boy whom neither would ultimately end up marrying. Speaking of the feud from an adult perspective, Hilary would say, 'It was weird because he caused all this trouble that I didn't really care about and that she couldn't have cared about. You're kids… what does it matter?' Aaron contended that he was an innocent victim in the feud. Years later Hilary commented, 'I didn't mean any harm if I dated him at the same time. I think he cheated on me, and I think he cheated on her… I love him to death as a friend, but he made it look like they had broken up.'

Hilary was obviously in love with Aaron at the time and would have done anything to keep him. 'Even though we dated when I was only 14, we did fall in love, and it was serious for us,' she later told a journalist. 'He did cheat on me, but whatever… We were 14. Who cares?'

Lindsay soon forgot about Aaron Carter, but her public arguments with Hilary continued. The second round of fighting took place at the première party for *Freaky Friday*, a few weeks after the *Vanity Fair* shoot. Lindsay was mortified when her on-screen love interest Chad Michael Murray invited Hilary to be his date. It was a painfully ironic twist and left Lindsay extremely red-faced. As it turned out, Hilary and Chad had just started filming *A Cinderella Story* together and were simply friends. When asked to compare the two girls, Chad laughed, 'They're so different, it's not even funny. They're two completely different human beings and two totally different actresses. They have different goals and concepts in their lives, but they're both sweethearts. That's the one thing I can say – they're both really cool and I get along with both of them.'

Several months after the encounter at the *Freaky Friday* première, Lindsay received an invitation from 20th Century Fox to the première of Hilary's new film *Cheaper by the Dozen*. Wanting to put an end to the past disharmony, Lindsay decided to attend. She was good friends with several of the other cast members and didn't want to miss out on a party.

When Lindsay arrived, she was relieved to spot her friends in the crowd and headed straight over to join a table with Ashton Kutcher. But not everyone was pleased to see Lindsay. Executives at 20th Century Fox didn't want to cause problems and insisted that Lindsay stay. She was their guest and she deserved to be present at the party. Lindsay had planned to leave quietly. Hilary and her mother eventually left early, as Hilary had to be up early for a flight to Boston the following morning. Lindsay, meanwhile, partied with her pals way into the night.

Later, Hilary would say she'd been totally oblivious to Lindsay's presence at the party. 'I couldn't even tell you what she looked like at the première. I think I've met her maybe twice. It's like every single time I see her she starts talking bad about me. She's so mean to me. It's sad.'

Hilary labelled the rivalry 'childish' and 'immature'. 'This all started because we both dated Aaron Carter, and she went around telling everybody that I was a horrible person who had stolen her boyfriend.' Hilary claimed Lindsay was also 'pissed off' about her friendship with Chad Michael Murray. 'She called him up and said all these awful things about me, which she then repeated to the press.' Hilary wished the rift would end. 'I don't think I can take it any more. It's so hurtful. Sometimes I feel like I really hate her, which is pretty extreme for me, because I don't hate anybody.'

The press continued to bait both girls into a full-scale public argument. Often, gossip stories would originate from a completely different source or would be misconstrued or taken totally out of context. All of this meant any form of reconciliation seemed totally out of the question. 'She's always trying to spread stories about me,' complained Hilary. 'But the funny thing is, I know so many stories about her that I could tell you right now! I'm not going to, because I don't think people should know and I don't want her to get mad at me for telling them.'

Although Hilary understandably was upset by the idea that somebody didn't like her: 'You know what the funny thing is in all this? I just want us to be friends – that's all.'

Lindsay couldn't agree more. 'I have no problem with her. Maybe she has a problem with me but I don't think she should. She doesn't need to do that. Her career is going great. People always make it seem worse than it is. The paparazzi and newspapers feed on girl actresses and any fight they can find or make up.'

Lindsay was beginning to realise that, while publicity was a benchmark of fame, it could equally result in an intrusion of privacy. This intuitive young woman was slowly learning the drawbacks of being a celebrity. 'Walking into a room, people just automatically think you're a certain way. That's the hardest part of this business. But, if you're comfortable with yourself, it will come through and people will say, "You're really not what I thought."'

Whether the public agreed with her version of events or not, everyone was in agreement that Lindsay Lohan was a fighter.

6

LEAN, MEAN, DRAMA QUEEN

Freaky Friday had been a defining point in Lindsay's career. Although she was already adept at being a young actress, she now had a celebrity profile to deal with. Fans who had watched the young star in *The Parent Trap* had grown up with Lindsay and had avidly followed her flourishing career. She'd now reached a new level of fame and it became more and more difficult to walk down the street without being recognised. 'I was walking past Mel's Diner and there were these little girls outside, and a billboard was right across the street,' she remembers. 'Everyone started looking and this one girl started whispering, "My God… that's Lindsay Lohan!"'

Fortunately, Lindsay's family and her co-stars had pre-warned her about the pitfalls of fame. While most girls her age would have been swept away by the attention, Lindsay managed to keep her feet firmly on the ground. She understood how fickle the world of celebrity could be and cared too much about her career to jeopardise her reputation by acting like a diva. 'My mom has led me in the right direction and made sure I was grounded and was in school when I needed to be and I think that's important.'

Lindsay didn't think that fame had changed her. For the most part, her friends still treated her in the same way, even though many of them were still freaked out by the attention she regularly received. 'People do recognise me more sometimes than they would have before *Freaky Friday*,' she confessed. 'I feel really honoured to be doing this and for people to be enjoying it. I just want to keep going for as long as I can.'

While filming *Freaky Friday*, Jamie Lee Curtis had advised Lindsay to keep smiling and enjoying her job. 'It's a lot of work,' she told Lindsay, obviously speaking from experience. 'It can get stressful and you get to a point where a lot of stuff is going on and it gets to you. Just make sure you're around good people.'

Dina had given Lindsay similar advice, telling her to carry on working as long as the job continued to be enjoyable.

Amid the furore of activity surrounding her private life, Lindsay managed to focus on her career and land more lucrative roles. Her third film was

Confessions of a Teenage Drama Queen, another light-hearted Disney comedy aimed at the pre-teen audience now doting on Lindsay. She was cast in the lead role of Lola, a native New Yorker who declares her life over when her family moves to the sticks of New Jersey. An immediate outcast, her wild stories and outrageous outfits fail to ingratiate Lola with her new classmates. Even more uproar ensues when she lands a lead role in the school play. 'I think everyone can relate to Lola, especially me!' said Lindsay, referring specifically to her own high-school switch. Making friends in new places hadn't been an easy experience.

She was also attracted to the message of the film, which would communicate directly to her younger audience. 'It's a really cute "believe in yourself" type of thing. If I can do something that's positive for younger kids – even girls my age – that's cute and fun, I might as well do it while I can. I'd like to stick with my audience for as long as I can, 'cause when you go forward you can't really go back.'

Although the role was more fantastical than anything she'd done previously, Lindsay enjoyed playing the outlandish character. She had more than 40 costume changes in the film and loved dressing up in different outfits. A varied wardrobe certainly maintained her interest and the physical requirements of switching set-ups so many times kept her energy levels high. 'It was fun to get all dolled up and dress like Marilyn Monroe,' she laughed.

Playing a teenage schoolgirl gave Lindsay ample opportunity to reflect on her own brief stint at high school. 'I look back and I hate how I was in seventh grade,' she says. 'I was so into pleasing everyone and dressing a certain way. It was like a huge fashion thing back then. We were in school with seniors and that was very intimidating. You grow up really fast when you're around older kids and I definitely went through a drama-queen phase. I'm still going through it!'

For the first time, Lindsay was also working alone. Working with a largely teenage cast, she lacked the adult mentors who had so carefully advised her on earlier films. 'I didn't have an adult there, I didn't have a Jamie. It was kinda more the pressure was on me.' But Lindsay relished the opportunity to work with actors her own age. While she would quite happily describe herself as being older than her years, essentially the young actress was still a teenage girl whose favourite topics of conversation were 'boys' and 'shopping'. 'I had a great time on the set. It was really fun to work with people my age because I'd never done that before.'

Another aspect of the film Lindsay found instantly appealing was the fact that her role would be a musical one. She contributed four songs to the *Confessions of a*

Teenage Drama Queen soundtrack, although the recordings were a lot poppier than her preferred style. She also enjoyed proving to audiences that she could dance. 'I wanted to show people two different sides.' But Lindsay was eager to stress that she wouldn't necessarily have a singing role in every movie she made from now on. 'It's not like I'm going to go singing in every movie I do. I just want to say that now, because then people are going to be like, "Well, does she need to sing in every movie to make the movie work?" It just so happened that there was singing in the script.'

Although an accomplished actress, Lindsay's ambitions didn't stop at the silver screen. Her main intention was to become a 'triple threat', a star capable of singing, dancing and acting. Among her idols, Lindsay counted Marilyn Monroe and Swedish-born star Ann-Margret. Both actresses had achieved Lindsay's goals in their lifetimes. Lindsay first become aware of Ann-Margret when people commented on her resemblance to the *Viva Las Vegas* star. But, after studying her career, Lindsay realised they had a lot more in common. 'I started researching her and watching her movies, and she seemed similar to me because she danced and was a singer and an actress,' she told interviewers.

Although *Confessions* met with a lukewarm response, Lindsay would go on to make another defining movie in her career. *Mean Girls* was scripted by *Saturday Night Live* writer Tina Fey and based on Rosalind Wiseman's book *Queen Bees & Wannabes: Helping Your Daughter Survive Cliques, Gossip, Boyfriends and Other Realities of Adolescence.*

Lindsay auditioned for the role of Cady, a 16-year old girl who is enrolled in high school for the first time after her zoologist parents return from a period spent living in the jungle. Very soon, she discovers that school is a jungle of a different sort. After befriending members of the 'out crowd', Cady encounters The Plastics – the coolest girls in school. Swept along by their elevated social status, she becomes an honorary member of the clan. But, when conflict ensues over a love interest, Cady plots to bring The Plastics down.

Lindsay instantly warmed to the script; not only was it hilarious but she could also easily identify with the tales of playground backstabbing common among girls in every American high school.

Originally, Lindsay wanted to play the role of head mean girl Regina, but had second thoughts at the last minute. 'I wanted to play the mean girl just to do something different, but I didn't want my audience to think I was actually mean!' Nevertheless, Lindsay enjoyed the transformations her character went through during the film. 'It's fun to change and it's more fun to play a character who goes through a transformation than to play someone who's static.'

Once again, Lindsay also enjoyed a series of dramatic costume changes, although she did object to certain outfits. 'I hated the days where I had to dress dowdy and all the other girls on set looked hot. I was like, "Ugggh!" But one time I had to wear this outfit that was like… nothing. It was a piece of fabric that was supposed to be a dress. I had all this make-up and black eyeliner on because it was supposed to show a dramatic change. It was fun but it was so overdone!'

Although *Mean Girls* reminded Lindsay of the fun she'd had at school, she felt relieved her days of classroom politics were over. 'In a way, this business – Hollywood – is a lot like high school. It's hard, but I'm close to my family and the friends that I have are my friends from first grade, and they haven't changed at all. They don't care about all this stuff and it's kept me who I am.'

Now a little older, Lindsay felt a lot more comfortable with herself and her own image. She attributed this newfound confidence to the hours spent on film sets working among adults. 'It's so much easier to wear no make-up now on set!' she laughed.

Lindsay had also grown more accustomed to filming kissing scenes. At first, she was worried about the off-screen relationship she'd share with her love interest in the film, Jonathan Bennett. 'It's always awkward when you're working with a guy who you have to be attracted to on set, because you start to like them,' she confessed at the time. 'Stuff like that always happens at my age. But we get along really well and it's on a good professional level.' Equally, Lindsay befriended other members of the cast and would regularly hang out with them off set.

Along with Tina Fey, several of the other *Saturday Night Live* cast members appeared in *Mean Girls*. Despite their almost iconic status, Lindsay wasn't at all frightened about working with them. 'It wasn't intimidating... it was fun,' she recalls. 'Tina was like, "I've never worked on a movie before. This is scary for me." Like, when she had her first day of shooting. And I was like, "No, no. We're gonna have fun. It will be awesome!" It was kinda cool that I was telling her that. We worked with each other. I was uncomfortable with some of the comedy that I had to do and she was just like, "Just go for it and have fun."'

No stranger to comedy, Lindsay enjoyed the elements of humour the *SNL* team brought to the set. 'They're all so funny. It's amazing to be around them.'

Returning the compliment, Tina Fey told magazines she would watch Lindsay to learn what it was really like to be a film actor. 'She never paraphrased a sentence once! She has this really quick-to-memorise spongy mind that you cannot have when you're 17.' But, at the same time, Tina recognised that Lindsay really was a teenager. 'She'd be on her pink cell phone calling her mom or online trying to track down a pair of baby-blue Ugg boots – which was obviously a few years ago because I know she wouldn't wear them now – and then they would say they were ready to shoot, and she would just turn and be fully present and really good in the scene. Then [they'd] call cut and she'd be like, "Anyway, I saw this thing…"'

Having survived the filming of *Confessions* without an adult mentor, Lindsay was learning to stand on her own two feet. Fortunately, she had a few familiar faces to help her along the way. Her old friend Mark Waters from *Freaky Friday* was also in charge of directing *Mean Girls*. He warned Lindsay she'd have to hold her own, be responsible and let people look up to her. Lindsay admitted she was scared. 'Before, I had adult actors I could turn to if I needed anything. Now it's different. With *Mean Girls*, I'm number one on the call sheet. But, if I do mess up here and there, I don't want people to think I'm immature on set and stuff.'

Mark didn't doubt her for a minute. 'She's growing up,' he said. 'She's just becoming a gorgeous young woman.'

Mean Girls opened at number one in the box office, leaving the much-hyped new Olsen twins' movie *New York Minute* trailing in its wake. It would gross over $86 million. 'This really puts her on the map as far as being a box-office draw,' said Paul Dergarabedian, president of the industry group Exhibitor Relations. His comments proved there was definitely a buzz about Lindsay in the business.

'This really affirms completely that she is a movie star,' said Paramount executive Rob Friedman. 'She's very, very savvy about what she's doing.'

While Lindsay was coming of age on screen, she was also beginning to make some mature decisions about her own life. Although she loved her family dearly, deep down Lindsay knew a move to Hollywood was gradually becoming essential to her career. Soon after her 17th birthday, she chose to take the plunge and move from New York to Los Angeles. Dina discussed joining her daughter but decided the upheaval would be unfair on her three other children who were still at school. It was a difficult choice to make. Dina couldn't help but worry that her eldest daughter was finally flying the nest. Although she would continue to work as Lindsay's manager, she could no longer assist her on a daily basis. Lindsay was also her best friend and it would be difficult to live without her. 'My parents went through this withdrawal phase when I told them,' said Lindsay. 'They were like, "You're not going to be living there full-time, right? You are going to be back and forth?" My mom was so afraid that I was going to move out and never talk to them again!'

Lindsay was secretly quite frightened about the move herself, but all parties agreed that it was a necessary step in her career. She was constantly being invited to auditions in LA and couldn't cope with the gruelling journeys for much longer. Besides, she was eager to explore a new place and meet more people in the film industry. Dina agreed to let her daughter go, but insisted that she hire an assistant who would act as a guardian and make sure she was taking good care of herself. Lindsay, meanwhile, had already found the perfect housemate. During the *Vanity Fair* shoot, she'd befriended actress Raven Symone, a former child star on *The Cosby Show* who now fronted her own Disney sitcom, *That's So Raven*. The two had a great deal in common; both had grown up quickly around adults and shared a mature outlook on life. Both girls had kept in regular contact since the shoot and Raven had mentioned to Lindsay that she was interested in renting a new apartment in LA. No sooner had Lindsay made her decision to relocate than she picked up the phone and dialled Raven's number. Dina could hear her daughter giggling excitedly in the room next door. She had met Raven on several occasions and thoroughly approved of her as a suitable friend. She smiled to herself; at least Lindsay would be in good company. 'She's so cool,' said Lindsay to Dina when she came off the phone.

'She's really honest and I like that. I think we'll mesh well.'

The size of their living space posed the first real problem. Raven suggested they rent a small apartment, as most of their time would probably be spent on film sets. She also enjoyed her privacy and wanted to discourage large parties of guests from dropping by. Lindsay, however, disagreed. 'I need people over,' she complained. 'I'll probably have friends over all the time. When Raven's not home, I won't sleep in the apartment alone. I don't like being home alone. I get scared. Besides, we need a bigger apartment because I can't fit anything in the closet!'

Finally, Raven conceded defeat and the girls opted for a larger apartment. In return, Lindsay agreed to leave all the decorating and colour schemes to Raven. The minute she stepped through the doorway, Raven was busy arranging decorators and selecting furnishings. Lindsay had only been in LA for a few days and her feet had hardly touched the ground. She was more than happy for her new flatmate to take control. As long as she had sufficient space to hang her clothes, that was all that really mattered. 'She really handled everything,' said Lindsay. 'She's been very mature. I think that's why we get along so well.'

As it turned out, Lindsay and Raven would hardly spend any time together as both were busy with film shoots and led very separate private lives. Ultimately,

Lindsay would move into her own place in August 2004. But, for now, she was looking forward to leading a glamorous Hollywood lifestyle. While her professional contact book would soon be bulging, her social calendar would be bursting at the seams. Joining the likes of Paris Hilton, Nicole Ritchie and the Olsen twins, Lindsay Lohan was fast becoming a Hollywood 'It' girl.

7

THE FAME GAME

Settling into a Hollywood lifestyle was quite overwhelming at first. In New York, Lindsay had found herself a comfortable niche; she was the international celebrity surrounded by a close network of friends. Now she felt as if she'd fallen right down to the bottom rung of the social ladder. In LA, everyone was a celebrity. She would need to fight hard to make her mark and become socially accepted by an entirely new crowd.

Fortunately, Lindsay already had several ready-made social networks in the city; she'd been travelling back and forth between LA and New York for years. But Lindsay was already prepared for several major changes to her lifestyle. In Merrick, she'd felt quite comfortable taking a stroll around the neighbourhood in her jogging bottoms. In LA, that would be deemed social suicide. Lindsay knew that Hollywood could be a breeding ground for vanity, but nothing could quite prepare her for the number of svelte, well-heeled women who would daily cross her path. Although Lindsay had learned to worry less about her appearance, she couldn't help but feel insecure. Even total unknowns dressed like international superstars. As a bona fide celebrity, Lindsay had a responsibility to look the part. One of her first missions when she arrived in LA was to hit the shops. After all, she'd worked hard and she deserved a treat.

Stepping outside her apartment, Lindsay hailed a cab downtown, nervously playing with her credit card. Although she could now command in excess of $1 million a movie, that amount of money still felt intangible in real terms. Spending money brings with it a certain amount of guilt, and Lindsay couldn't kick her pragmatic conscience.

Her first port of call was a jewellery store. Fed up with dull and forgettable accessories, Lindsay wanted to splash out on something special. If she was going to be earning a million dollars, she may as well look the part. Once inside the store, she quickly found all the justification she required to flex her purchasing power. Glancing at small trinkets and charm bracelets, she was suddenly distracted by a diamond-encrusted Chopard watch, shimmering beneath the store lights. The price tag read $80,000, but it was only a fraction of her wage packet from *Mean Girls*. Lindsay had already made up her mind. 'I think I deserve this watch,' she said under her breath. Lindsay Lohan had arrived in Tinseltown.

Of course, Lindsay's purchases were never always that extravagant. 'I'd draw the line at a Dior dog collar,' she later joked to a friend. During the same shopping trip, Lindsay had been tempted to buy a Fendi satin-and-rhinestone eye patch for sleeping, but couldn't justify the asking price. 'It was $500! You've got to be kidding. That's disgusting.' But, before long, Lindsay's closets in New York and LA were overflowing with clothes and accessories. Vintage clothes stores – such as Resurrection in LA and What Comes Around Goes Around in Manhattan – quickly became her favourite haunts. 'It's dangerous,' she would later say, referring to her insatiable shopping addiction. She was also a hoarder and refused to throw anything away. 'I always get yelled at, but when you're travelling so much you're living out of a suitcase, so you don't take the time to hang everything up and look at what you have.'

Kelly Osbourne would later joke about Lindsay's indecision in picking an outfit. 'The only person I know who takes longer than me is Lindsay Lohan. We went to a Rolling Stones show during Fashion Week and she changed, like, 15 times!'

At the time, Lindsay's style was a mix 'n' match of fashions. She hadn't yet determined exactly how she liked to dress. 'My style changes all the time,' she shrugged. 'It might be jeans with stilettos or a little skirt with a Chrome Hearts tank top and a pair of Uggs.' Lindsay admitted she went through phases and dressed depending on her mood that day. 'I change... I dress all vintage one day and hip-hop the next.'

Lindsay also spent a fair amount of time on her hair and make-up. She was actually born with wavy hair, but preferred to straighten it. 'My hair's wavy, but I feel cleaner when it's straight,' she explained. Lindsay cited *Friends* star Jennifer Aniston as her fashion icon, because she never made fashion mistakes. Lindsay loved her classy but fun, down-to-earth style. It was an image she hoped to emulate. One look Lindsay really despised, however, was 'denim on denim'. 'I made the mistake of saying that to [US talk-show host] Jay Leno!' she laughed. 'He asked me what someone should never wear and I said denim on denim. It's my pet peeve. He wears denim on denim every day to work before he goes on TV and I was like, "Oh my God! I did not just say that!"'

While Lindsay was taking to her new glamorous lifestyle like a duck to water, she still harboured an unaffected, down-to-earth quality at the core of her character. 'She's so real. She's so honest. Raw. I think that's what America loves about her,' declared Dina on her daughter's phenomenal success.

Lindsay knew it was important to stay in touch with her real friends from New York who had lent their support since the beginning of her career. During the time she'd spent on various film sets, she'd witnessed numerous young actors become dangerously self-obsessed. She was determined never to fall into a similar trap herself.

While Lindsay had admittedly grown up quickly, she still made an effort to engage in normal teenage activities. Often she'd invite her friends to film premières or simply hang out at the local shopping mall. She had the best of both worlds; she could enjoy being an international film star while still acting like a normal teen. 'A lot of my friends are still at high school,' she claimed. 'I hang out with them and do normal things. I've learned to focus on things that make me happy.'

Even though Lindsay was now a fully fledged Hollywood star, she didn't feel any different inside. 'I don't think I have personally changed, and my friends haven't changed, but sometimes people do recognise me more. That's a great feeling.' Even now, Lindsay admits she feels honoured and blessed to be so successful in her chosen profession. 'I want to keep doing this for as long as I can.' But, in fact, she often felt uncomfortable with her newly elevated social status. While walking past a newsstand one day, she happened to glance over and catch her face on a magazine cover. She read the headline: 'LINDSAY LOHAN – MOVIE STAR'. The thought made her shudder. 'I don't like it when people use those words to describe me,' she explains. 'It's a compliment, and I'm completely honoured that someone would say that about me, but I don't want people thinking I'm any different to anyone else. People say to me now that I'm a celebrity, a movie star, but that's scary,' she complained modestly. 'I don't think I'm at that place yet. I don't think I deserve that yet. I've done movies but I haven't really shown enough of a change in my characters to really gain that respect.'

In fact, Lindsay often felt awkward around her new legion of fans. 'I don't feel like I have any power,' she confessed, not wanting people to think she was some kind of self-obsessed megalomaniac. 'I've been working hard and trying to get to this position, and I feel like people are starting to recognise the stuff that I'm doing, and enjoying it. It makes me feel really good when my little sister and her friends peek inside my bedroom door and stare at me. It's cool to have people look up to you. But I'm not in a position yet where I can just be like, "Oh, I want to do this kind of movie."'

But, no matter how much she tried to deny it, Lindsay *was* very different to everyone else. Even in the celebrity Mecca of LA, she was finding it harder to remain anonymous. Dark glasses and baseball caps did little to disguise the rising star. The freckles and red hair that Lindsay had once so fervently despised were now becoming a clearly distinguishable identity tag. On one occasion, Lindsay invited a group of New York school friends to visit her in LA during the summer break. She had been missing her friends desperately, so when a window appeared in her schedule she eagerly seized it and set aside time for her pals. She wanted to show them the sights of her new hometown, and decided lunch followed by a shopping trip would make the perfect day out.

The girls were in awe of Lindsay's new glamorous lifestyle. Wandering around her apartment, they couldn't believe the number of new gadgets she'd acquired. A tour of her well-stocked wardrobe took almost an hour. Before long, there were piles of designer garments all over Lindsay's bed. Feeling a little guilty about her expenditure, she even gave away a few items to her extremely grateful friends. If she were really honest with herself, there were clothes in that wardrobe she couldn't even recall buying. In exchange for her generosity, her friends filled her in on all the gossip she'd missed out on in New York.

Eventually, the girls managed to prise themselves away from Lindsay's wardrobe. Their anxious host was already conscious time was brief and there was some serious shopping to be done. Armed with credit cards and ready for action, the girls set off on a boutique trawl. At some point during the afternoon, however, the paparazzi were tipped off that Lindsay was out and about in town. Lindsay had become so accustomed to their daily request for a photograph that she hadn't even stopped to think they might harass her friends as well. The girls were selecting outfits from a boutique on Robertson Boulevard when a swarm of photographers suddenly descended upon them. At first, Lindsay noticed only one camera flash, but before long there were about a dozen paparazzi peering in through the shop window. Lindsay quickly ushered her stunned friends towards a car. None of them really knew quite what to make of all the commotion. A few were even frightened by the insistent requests for a smile. 'I felt so bad for my friends,' complained Lindsay afterwards. 'You literally could not see out the windows because they were filled with guys in black shirts taking pictures.'

It became obvious that Lindsay would have to watch her moves carefully – before long, even a trip to the corner shop would be splashed across a magazine spread. On a separate occasion, Lindsay wanted to drop by fast-food restaurant Wendy's with some friends. At the time, five cars of paparazzi were hot on her tail. 'I wanted to stop at Wendy's,' she later recalled. 'My friend was like, "You don't want them to take your picture there. It'll be, 'They eat like us!'" so I ducked down when we went through the drive-through.'

For the time being, Lindsay had learned to deal with the paparazzi. She was accustomed to having her photo taken in public and knew it was far easier simply to smile and wave rather than run away and act aggressively. 'Of course it's weird when you're leaving your hotel or wherever and having people following you just to get a picture,' she confessed. 'But this is something I've always aspired to do and I love it!'

On further reflection, Lindsay would laugh, 'I think it's so cool they want my picture! It's kinda weird, but it's cool.' She appreciated that, while photographers could occasionally be intrusive, they were simply responding to public demand. As long as the press wanted to feature Lindsay's picture, she could be sure the public were still interested in her career. 'It's a really great feeling to know that people are going to go and see a movie if they see my picture and know I'm in it,' she said with genuine enthusiasm. She'd spent her whole life looking up to actresses in a similar position, so to be finally experiencing the same thing was quite an amazing feeling.

Unfortunately, the attention Lindsay received was not always welcome. Lindsay already had a keen male following and was now regarded as a pin-up.

As she grew older, the demographic of her fan base was changing. Whereas little girls had once trailed her for an autograph, now she was being followed by grown men. Disturbingly, some of them didn't know when to give up. One particular fan became so obsessed with Lindsay that he pursued her wherever she went. Although she found it flattering at first, the fiery redhead soon lost her temper when 'AJ' (as he became known) became a pest. Whether she was in a restaurant with friends, posing for a photo shoot or in transit between auditions, he never seemed further than two steps behind Lindsay. Often, she would lie in bed at night wondering if he might try to break into her house. Any person who would dedicate their whole life to keeping tabs on a person they had never met had to be mentally imbalanced.

Initially, Lindsay was reluctant to discuss the matter with Dina for fear she would fret unnecessarily. Instead, she confined any fears to the pages of her private journal. But, eventually, Dina found out. Distraught with worry, she begged Lindsay to go straight to the police. But Lindsay had a heart of gold and didn't want to land anyone in trouble. Although she was frightened, she felt a little sorry for AJ. She simply closed her eyes and wished he'd go away – more for his sake, than her own.

Tolerant for so long, Lindsay finally snapped

Lindsay and co-star Jamie Lee Curtis at the premiere of *Freaky Friday* – the film which cemented her Hollywood reputation – in LA.

Above left: Lindsay with her mother Dina.

Above right: With her younger siblings – sister Aliana, and brother Dakota.

Bottom: A scene from *Confessions of a Teenage Drama Queen* – Lindsay enjoyed proving to audiences that she could sing and dance as well as act.

Lindsay at the *Mean Girls* premiere with the writer of the film, and star of *Saturday Night Live,* Tina Fey. The success of *Mean Girls* catapulted Lindsay into the Hollywood A-list, where she could command huge fees for films.

Lindsay's father is arrested again, in yet another incident to bring unwanted media attention upon the Lohans.

Despite personal turmoil with her father, the success of *Mean Girls* meant demand for Lindsay had never been higher.

Above left: At the 2004 MTV Movie Awards – Lindsay was the youngest ever presenter.

Above right: Presenting the MTV TRL Music Awards.

Below: Lindsay was invited to indulge her gift for comedy, this time on the small screen, on *Saturday Night Live*.

Enjoying the trappings of a movie-star lifestyle as a Hollywood 'It' girl…

Above: With Nicole Richie and Nicky Hilton (Paris Hilton's sister).

Below: With Kelly Osbourne and Mary Kate Olsen.

Doing what she loves – shopping with socialite Paris Hilton.

Lindsay at the Latin Grammy Awards with her first true love – television star Wilmer Valderrama.

during her friend Wilmer Valderrama's 24th birthday party. AJ had attempted to crash the party in a desperate bid to meet the object of his affections, but the bouncers had refused him entry. Lindsay had warned most of the clubs in LA to keep him away. Disgruntled, he sought revenge by contacting the police to report Lindsay for underage drinking. The police arrived at the party to question Lindsay, causing her much distress and embarrassment. Although she had been drinking fruit juice all evening, she was still frightened she might end up in a police cell, and she dreaded what the tabloids might make of that. But, worst of all, she felt bad for ruining her friend's birthday.

Other guests at the party felt extremely uncomfortable with officers in the building. It had been an abrupt intrusion. After questioning Lindsay for a lengthy period, the police were satisfied that she hadn't broken the law. She was relieved, but now she had an even greater problem to deal with – a stalker who would go to any lengths to make contact with her. Fearful for her safety, Lindsay's guardian and assistant Leslie Sloane Zelnik suggested she seek a restraining order against AJ.

But AJ wasn't the first person to draw unwanted attention to Lindsay's party lifestyle. Media fascination with her private life was steadily growing and the press focused a disproportionate amount of attention on Lindsay's social activities, glossing over any work commitments she might be keeping during the day. Tales of a Disney role model with a taste for the wild side were instant headline-grabbers.

In truth, Lindsay was behaving no differently to any other average American teen. Her only real crime was to grow up in the public eye. While Lindsay was committed to working hard on set, she liked to unwind with friends by dancing in clubs and socialising with other young people in her industry. With so many invitations arriving on her doorstep daily, it would be stupid to reject every one and stay indoors. Rather than frown disapprovingly, Dina agreed her daughter should be making the most of every opportunity. 'I didn't raise Lindsay up to sit at home!' she laughed when quizzed by reporters.

As the child star grew into a young woman, her physical attributes were frequently discussed in the press. One of the most hurtful rumours suggested Lindsay had been under the plastic surgeon's knife. The obsessively self-conscious star already had plenty of issues with her body image. 'I'm always making fun of myself. I don't like how I look. My face is too fat,' she would complain to Dina. 'That's how I am – I have to get more confident with myself. I'm always saying, "I want to have blonder hair... I wish I didn't have freckles... I wish I had naturally darker skin..." Stuff like that. I wish I'd just stop that because I annoy myself when I say that. That's what I have to do now.'

Bizarrely, Lindsay took comfort in beating herself up and, at the very least, that sort of self-criticism kept her ego in check. 'I think my insecurities benefit me in a lot of ways, because [they keep] me grounded.'

But the tabloids didn't harp on Lindsay's looks per se, rather on her well-developed cleavage. The topic of Lindsay's breasts became an international debate – were they real or had they been cosmetically enhanced? More than anyone, Lindsay was amazed by the amount of attention her assets were attracting. Although deeply offended by the suggestion she'd had surgery, she tried to laugh it off. 'Recently, I heard that I've gotten a boob job. I'm 17!' she exclaimed. 'It's so retarded. My mother would never let me. I'd be deathly afraid, and it's unnecessary. I would never get implants, ever.'

Throughout her adolescence, Lindsay had been patiently waiting for her chest to grow. All her other friends seemed to develop at a faster rate and she felt quite inadequate in comparison. As a child, she had even used toilet tissue to pad out her T-shirts. When her breasts finally did make an appearance, they did it with aplomb. 'I just got my chest in the past year, and I couldn't be happier,' she gushed. 'I used to be the flattest person ever, stuffing my bras.' And Lindsay was willing to admit her boobs had grown at an alarming rate. 'I will admit that, when I first started to develop boobs, my friends were like, "Oh my God, what happened, and are your boobs real?" Even me, I was in shock because I was so flat that, when I got a chest, it was like, wow. And compared to the rest of my body they kind of, like, popped. And they sit up. But I'm young and I only just got my boobs, so of course they're going to look good. I love 'em!'

However, a proliferation of websites dedicated to her cleavage did make Lindsay feel uncomfortable. Close-up shots of her chest would appear in magazines and some even ran public-opinion polls on the topic. Disney wardrobe assistants were careful to dress their young star appropriately, concerned her shapely features weren't exactly the ideal focal point for a family-orientated film. 'It's kind of perverted, but, if they're gonna write about anything to bring attention to my chest, why not!' Lindsay once even admitted she enjoyed reading the more obscene stories about herself, 'because you know what's true and what's not'.

While Lindsay could often shrug off stories as nonsense, it was the impact on her family she really found upsetting. One day she received a distressed phone call from her younger sister Aliana. Having just turned 13, Ali was at an impressionable age where tabloid tales were often taken to be gospel truths. Everyone at school read gossip magazines and, at first, Ali was proud to have an A-list sister who regularly featured. But certain stories upset her. Other schoolchildren would taunt her with cruel headlines and scandalous revelations. Ali admired Lindsay more than anyone else in the world. She hated to think the rest of the world knew more about Lindsay than she did.

Particularly distressed at the stories of her big sister's alleged boob job, she phoned up Lindsay and demanded the truth. 'I heard you got Pamela Anderson boobs,' she screamed to Lindsay down the phone.

Thankfully, Dina intervened to calm her youngest daughter down. She blamed the press for causing so much upset. Rolling her eyes at all the unnecessary commotion, Dina sensibly pointed out that puberty was the only explanation for her daughter's larger bust. 'Lindsay's at a very tender age. You know, she grew,' she said, cupping her hands to her chest. 'They're real, by the way.'

All the additional press attention began to irritate Lindsay. While she didn't mind posing for photographers at promotional engagements or even out and about during her normal routine, she resented their constant intrusion into her social life. After hours, Lindsay craved some normality. The increasingly disillusioned teen was under the impression that an unspoken deal had been brokered; if she smiled sweetly and allowed a few shots, the paparazzi would leave her in peace. Surely her previous compliance with their requests demanded some kind of respect? But Lindsay Lohan was already hot property and, in the eyes of the press, she represented dollar signs. No matter what, they refused to leave her alone.

Aged only 17, Lindsay was still considered a minor in the state of California and four years below the legal drinking limit. But already she'd earned notoriety as a regular face on the club circuit. The press were desperate to catch a shot of the young star stumbling out of one of Hollywood's well-known nightspots. Gossip columnists would recount endless tales of outrageous behaviour, often inferring that alcohol was involved. Lindsay grew exasperated at having to defend herself. 'When my friends and I go out, we just get a table and observe what goes on,' she pleaded. 'We're calm. We know our place. We don't have to get stupid and drunk – we can have fun without drinking.' After all, why would she be stupid enough to jeopardise her career by drinking in full public view of a watchful crowd ready to pounce? 'If I wanted to drink, I'd stay home and do it with my friends,' she said with a wry smile. 'If I go to a club, I'm not going to come out of it trashed. I'd rather stay home with my friends if I was going to do that – especially if you know there are going to be 20 guys with cameras waiting for you outside. In this business, you come to understand that there are going to be pictures taken of you and you learn what goes along with that.'

Lindsay had already proven herself to be an extremely affable character and quickly made friends on LA's party scene. She hung out with a celebrity crowd, including the likes of Paris Hilton, Nicole Ritchie and the Olsen twins. She also had several older friends in the industry. Most of them were sympathetic to her situation and plenty of the more reputable nightclub bosses exercised a certain amount of discretion over her presence in their clubs. Preferring her to make an inconspicuous entrance, many of them would usher Lindsay in through the back door. Technically, she never broke the law. 'I know all the guys who own the clubs. We made a deal where they let me come in and I'll drink only Red Bull,' she claimed.

But creeping around furtively often left Lindsay feeling frustrated. 'It's hard being 17 years old and not able to do the same things that other 17-year-olds do,' she sighed to Dina. Lindsay was slowly learning the complicated rules of Hollywood and she didn't like them one little bit. Whenever her friends from New York came down to visit, they were desperate to sample the high life they'd read about in magazines. Always the obliging host, Lindsay didn't want to disappoint them. She recalls one particular occasion: 'I had some friends in town recently on spring break.

They wanted to go out every night, and I wanted to show them a good time. So I took them out, and the paparazzi started taking pictures of me.' Now an old hand at this kind of thing, Lindsay brushed the incident aside.

The following morning, however, her publicist received a phone call from the tabloids. 'We're going to write a story on Lindsay, and we're going to call her the new "It" party girl!' they warned.

Lindsay was furious. 'Just because I'm 17 and I'm having fun, they start saying I'm trying to be older, partying and going crazy,' she complained. 'I don't even like to drink!'

Then there were the love interests. Lindsay had already confessed in interviews to having a crush on stars such as Jude Law and Lothario Colin Farrell. Having grown up so quickly herself, she was naturally attracted to older men. 'It's easier for me, maturity-wise, to talk to them,' she explained, referring to the adult responsibilities she dealt with on a daily basis. 'I've been doing this for so long and I've grown up around adults, and I've had a lot of responsibilities my whole life, so I've had to mature faster and be more focused. I feel like I'm a lot older than I am. My friends are much older than me. I work a lot and I have a job every day, and people my age don't understand that. So it's hard, but I wouldn't have it any other way.'

When Lindsay heard Colin Farrell was in LA shooting for a new film, she made no secret of her adoration for the hell-raiser. 'Colin Farrell is in town? He's really cool,' she told one journalist, with a cheeky grin. Lindsay was already a self-confessed flirt, a talent she'd inherited from her mother and, when she set her sights on a man, she usually got him. One rumour suggested she'd actually propositioned the Irish actor at Paramount Studios. She fervently denied that any such meeting had taken place, however. The story alleged that 27-year-old Colin had called off a date with Lindsay after discovering that she was only 17. Lindsay claimed the story was nonsense. 'I actually wasn't even on the studio lot when the press said I did that,' she protested. 'I met him at a friend's house for the first time after all that happened. It's so ridiculous.' A year later, however, Lindsay would confess the pair 'hung out at a club' and may have shared an intimate moment. 'I guess we were spotted kissing. But it wasn't such a bad rumour to have.'

Apart from the obvious personal stress such claims were causing Lindsay, they also had dangerous implications for her professional career. Disney would not be happy to read stories of their young star drunkenly stumbling between clubs with a different man on her arm every night. She also had a younger fan base to consider, many of whom looked up to her as a role model. It was an incredible responsibility to bear. 'Disney are very protective of our relationship,' she explained. 'It's kind of like old Hollywood – they guide your career. It's hard to see Mischa [Barton from *The OC*] and the other girls who can go out and get away with things. Most kids my age do drink, but you'll usually see them when it's an event or an after-party where there's not an age limit. If I'm at an after-party, I'm always with my guardian. I don't want to have a drink and have someone whip out a camera-phone and Disney getting it. It's not worth it. I don't want to risk my career for a night of having fun.'

If Lindsay had to name one drawback to being a celebrity, it's that people always expect her to be the way they imagine her. 'That's the hardest part of being in this business. When you walk into a room, people just automatically think you're a certain way. But, if you're comfortable with yourself, it will come through and people will say, "You're really not what I thought."'

It was easy to see how people could become confused. With so many stories arising daily, the line between fact and fiction could easily be blurred. Lindsay only had so much time in her day to refute allegations and she often had to let things go. Hopefully, the people who really counted would be sensible enough to judge the star at face value.

Those who didn't probably weren't worth knowing in the first place.

Whenever Lindsay became too wound up about the situation, she had to take a step back and consider how ridiculous the rumours were actually becoming. In truth, her social life was a lot less lively than many other teens her age; she simply didn't have the time in her schedule to be a Hollywood 'It' girl. 'I don't go out that much!' she laughed. 'People just say I do.' Usually, she was tucked up in bed by 1.00am having watched a bit of TV. 'I usually have *Sex and the City* on. That puts me to sleep!' Slightly ashamed, Lindsay admits she already owns every DVD from the series. 'I watch it because I am basically obsessed with Sarah Jessica Parker. She is so similar to her character, and I relate to Carrie Bradshaw – I love her style, and she always goes through the guy problems – just like me.'

Although she didn't like it, Lindsay knew she'd become unwittingly involved in the fame game. Often the only way to communicate directly with her fans was through the press. It was just unfortunate journalists didn't always represent the truth. 'They say a lot of things,' she sighed. 'The thing is, these magazines take pictures and young girls buy them. So it leads to them wanting to get more pictures so they can sell more magazines. I guess it makes sense from a business standpoint.'

For now, Lindsay could forgive the press, but soon her patience would wear thin. Eventually, her party antics would become yesterday's news and the paparazzi would direct their attention elsewhere. Once Lindsay had settled into her new Hollywood lifestyle, she hoped the commotion surrounding her arrival would calm down. Besides, soon the gossip columnists would have some new material to sink their teeth into – Lindsay's first serious boyfriend.

8

BOYED UP

While Lindsay had made plenty of new friends in LA, she still hankered after the close-knit community of pals she'd grown up with in New York. Bonds that have developed over time can't necessarily be recreated overnight. Although Dina continued to manage her daughter and would regularly commute between LA and New York, Lindsay missed her guiding hand. While they continued to speak every day, intimate conversations would now take place over the phone rather than downstairs in the kitchen with a cup of coffee. She also missed her younger siblings and, whereas once she'd dreaded babysitting chores, she now secretly longed for the opportunity. 'I babysat my brother and sister, and it was the worst time ever because they would not stop fighting. They were killing each other!' she later recalled. 'I ended up locking my sister out of the house for, like, two seconds. But I love being around them.' It might seem incongruous with all the press attention she was receiving, but, away from the eagle-eyed crowds watching her every move, Lindsay Lohan was lonely.

The transition to a Hollywood lifestyle had been difficult and Lindsay battled with nagging insecurities on a daily basis. Appearing outwardly confident, inside she would constantly question her worth. Deep down, she wondered whether she could actually cope with all the added pressures fame was exerting on her. Hollywood was oversaturated with beautiful blonde and skinny women. In comparison, the freckled redhead felt like an outsider.

Already confident in her abilities as an actress, Lindsay needed a boost in her private life. Desperate for closeness and intimacy, she needed a boyfriend. 'I think the best thing for someone my age, the best thing that I need right now, just to keep me grounded, is a boyfriend,' she declared one day. After much thought, Lindsay had reached the conclusion that a steady boyfriend would tame her wild image in the press. 'Going out a lot gives people the wrong impression of you,' she claimed. 'If you have a boyfriend, you have a reason to stay home a lot, and you have someone to talk to.'

Lindsay was determined to find herself a man. All she faced now was the logistical problem of actually hunting one down. Operating in a world of drop-dead-gorgeous pin-ups would be every young girl's dream, but Lindsay generally preferred to maintain a professional relationship with her co-stars. 'It's hard when you're looking for a boyfriend,' she complained. 'When you're looking for someone, you're not going to find them.' To make matters worse, Lindsay often felt intimidated when in new company. 'I think it's because I'm very honest,' she said with a degree of self-reflection. 'I always speak my mind. If you're bothering me or doing something that's offensive to me, I'm going to tell you rather than talk about you behind your back. But, if I don't know you yet, I can be very shy.'

When Lindsay met Venezuelan-born actor Wilmer Valderrama, better known as Fez from *That '70s Show*, she instantly knew her search had come to an end. Blessed with dark and brooding Latin features, Wilmer was gorgeous. Lindsay couldn't help but admire his laidback and reserved demeanour. The fact that he was 24 (roughly six years her senior) proved even more appealing. Wilmer had already dated several high-profile women, including Jennifer Love Hewitt and Mandy Moore, but currently he was single. As her close friends would later testify, Lindsay was smitten. She would keep tabs on his social engagements and, wherever possible, make sure she was in attendance. Being a traditional girl at heart, Lindsay waited for Wilmer to ask her out. 'Of course I waited for him to make the first move!' she confessed. 'A girl should never do that!'

The pair shared mutual friends, so Lindsay had no problem in letting it be known she felt an attraction. She would frequently glance over in Wilmer's direction, before quickly looking away and acting coy. When the pair finally spoke, they instantly hit it off. Wilmer admired Lindsay's strength and independence. She was a born achiever who set her sights high. Equally, he felt drawn to the playful and carefree sides of her character. She was a good-natured and loving soul. So few girls in Hollywood were capable of expressing their emotions; with Lindsay, they flowed so naturally.

Lindsay has always felt comfortable around older men. 'But it's not like I'm going to date a 30-year-old!' she said jokingly, before adding, 'Unless it's Jude Law! My parents and I have an agreement that dating him would be OK!'

Wilmer possessed qualities so glaringly absent in boys Lindsay's own age – he was confident, assured and intelligent. The fawning teen was thrilled to accept a date.

Unfortunately, not everyone agreed with Lindsay's views on older men – particularly the California State Police Department. Lindsay was still below the legal age of consent and the last thing she needed was more controversy in the press. For that very reason, the couple decided to keep their fledgling relationship under wraps for the time being. It actually gave Lindsay a great excuse to stay indoors and take a break from the party circuit. The pair would often order take-out and cuddle up together on the sofa in front of a DVD. After a long and difficult day at the studio, there was no place Lindsay would rather be than in her boyfriend's arms. She was desperate to show Wilmer off to the world, but equally enjoyed spending time with him away from the media circus. 'He's a great guy!' she enthused to close friends. 'I love him to death. We've become really, really good friends. Seriously, I think he's one of the best guys any girl could be with. He's really sweet. It's very fun.'

Falling in love for the first time gave Lindsay the opportunity to reflect on her only other high-profile boyfriend, Aaron Carter. Now faced with the real thing, she knew her past liaisons had been nothing more than puppy love. Confident in that knowledge, she felt comfortable discussing her childhood sweetheart with the press. 'Aaron and I are good friends,' she said diplomatically. 'We did date in the past, but it's, like, a personal thing, you know what I mean?' With the relationship locked safely in the past, she no longer needed to worry about alienating female fans. 'People are going to find out. We have to expect that, and you have to make the best of it.'

In the past, Dina had advised her daughter against divulging details of the relationship with Aaron. She was concerned about a potential backlash from jealous female fans. However, Lindsay now felt confident her fans would respond sympathetically. After all, wouldn't any girl have done the same in her position?

Regardless, Lindsay had moved on. Initially, she was worried about introducing Wilmer to her mother, whose opinion she valued dearly. But, like her daughter, Dina was instantly bowled over by Wilmer's charm and sense of humour. As far as she was concerned, he ticked all the right boxes in the boyfriend department. 'Wilmer is an angel,' she assured Lindsay over the phone. 'I just love him to death. He's a sweetheart, an old soul and a really great boy.'

Early signs were already indicating that Lindsay had found her first serious boyfriend. Although Dina had never doubted her daughter's ability to look after herself, she was relieved to see Lindsay settle down with a man she thoroughly approved of. 'He's very protective of Lindsay,' she proudly boasted to friends.

It was only a matter of time before Lindsay became desperate to share her happiness with fans. Like any girl in love for the first time, she wanted everyone to know. Besides, in a town where photographers lurk at every corner, keeping the love affair under wraps was tough. The pair had already been spotted taking a romantic stroll together, causing an eruption of rumours in the press. Wilmer was also upset by numerous tabloid reports linking Lindsay with other men, the latest of which had Mary-Kate Olsen's ex Matt Kaplan down as her beau. Lindsay and Wilmer both knew it was time to come clean.

The couple decided that Lindsay's 18th birthday party would be the ideal opportunity to go public with their relationship. But the last thing the tabloid-taunted actress wanted was a horde of photographers on her doorstep. Knowing the press would be expecting a star-studded and lavish event, she tried to throw them off the scent by playing down any plans she might have. 'It'll just be a few close friends,' she told *Rolling Stone* magazine in an interview. 'We'll get dinner and then... I don't know. Everyone will probably be tired and just go home.' It didn't take a genius to detect the note of sarcasm in her voice. As if party-loving Lindsay would let her coming of age pass by with a whimper! Secretly, she had made plans for a party at swanky LA nightspot Avalon, to take place on 2 July 2004. A guest list of names was hurriedly compiled, reading like a *Who's Who* of young Hollywood. Those lucky enough to receive an invite included Tara Reid, the Hilton sisters and the Olsens.

The party was a glamorous affair with an 'I'm A Slave 4 You' theme. Characteristically excitable, Lindsay was bursting with energy. Flinging her arms wide open, she greeted her guests with rapturous enthusiasm. Clearly in her element, she took the chance to dance with all of them. Most of her attention, however, was reserved for Wilmer. Their very public displays of affection left no one doubting that the love-struck pair were an item. At one point, Lindsay dashed over to the DJ booth and requested 'Stand Up' by Ludacris. No sooner had the track kicked in than she grabbed Wilmer for some seriously sexy grinding. 'He's a really great dancer!' she boasted to friends. 'I think any girl would be lucky to date him.'

They created quite a spectacle, with some bystanders even offering applause. 'She is my girl,' Wilmer told everyone. 'I love her very much. She is a fantastic person and I'm extremely proud of her.'

When friends asked the star how it felt to be 18,

she replied, 'It doesn't feel much different. It is kind of weird because people are like, "Oh, you are 18 now, how do you feel?" I mean, now I can talk to guys that are 21 without people saying it's bad!'

The freedom to express her feelings for Wilmer in public was the best present anyone could have given Lindsay. The couple were utterly devoted to each other and their relationship was now something Lindsay could be proud of. Earlier in the evening, the pair had exchanged promise rings as a sign of their affection. This was definitely a defining point in their relationship and a pledge of commitment to each other. Taking full advantage of their newfound freedom, the pair partied until 3.00am.

Soon after Lindsay's birthday, the love-struck pair took a two-week holiday in Miami. The past few months had been difficult for the young stars and they both needed to escape the Hollywood limelight. Lindsay and Wilmer made the most of an opportunity to kick back and relax while working on their tans. Whereas in the past Lindsay had sheltered in the shade for fear of her freckles flaring up, she no longer really cared. 'I never thought, at 18, that I'd wake up in the morning with someone that I'd like and not care if my breath smells,' she said of the relationship. 'This is my first boyfriend... and it's cool.'

Relatively inexperienced in the realm of relationships, Lindsay was frightened by the intensity of her emotions. 'I've gotten feelings toward him really fast, which I'm not used to,' she confessed. Whenever possible, she jumped at the chance to talk about Wilmer. He had become such a huge part of her life, and every decision she now made revolved around him. In interviews, she would talk freely about the relationship, but still remained coy about the finer and more intimate details. When one TV presenter asked whether Wilmer was a good kisser, Lindsay recoiled with embarrassment. 'I don't know... I don't know. I have a ten-year-old sister who might be watching this!'

Despite her reluctance to divulge information, Lindsay managed to spark rumours of marriage by boasting of how she'd love to be a young mum. 'My mom was a young mom, and it was cool to have that because she was my friend growing up,' she explained. Such grand admissions could quite easily land Lindsay in trouble. Her publicist quickly stepped in to play down any speculation that she might be tying the knot and friends advised the lovestruck teen to tread carefully. Professionally, she'd reached a crucial point in her life and her career had to take priority. Lindsay took note, but she wasn't really interested. As far as the naive 18-year-old was concerned, life could be no better;

she'd finally found the emotional crutch she'd been so desperately seeking.

As the events of future months unfolded, her discovery would prove fortuitous. Very soon, Lindsay Lohan would need someone to lean on.

9

THE SINS OF THE FATHER

While Lindsay appeared to bathe in the glory of her new LA lifestyle, back home in New York the Lohan family strife continued. Her father's four-year prison term in the '90s marked the beginning of a series of run-ins with the police. His personal problems continued, amid allegations of temper tantrums. Dina tried desperately hard to protect her children from the marital problems, but inevitably they became inextricably involved.

In 2000, Dina requested a protection order against Michael after filing for divorce. He then phoned his estranged wife 150 times in a 24-hour period, prompting her to phone the police and resulting in a second prison term. Although Lindsay was now comfortably removed from the situation, she couldn't help but worry about her family. For all her father's misdemeanours, deep down she still loved him. But hiding her past from the press was becoming impossible. 'The situation is a sore subject,' she would later say. 'I'm a normal girl and I have normal stuff that goes on in my life and that's really all there is to it.'

Michael's alleged behaviour was pure tabloid fodder and he wasn't shy of discussing his family's woes in public. The last thing Lindsay needed was more press attention, but she had little control over the situation. Michael Lohan was about to become a celebrity in his own right.

In May 2004, Lindsay travelled back to New York to celebrate her seven-year-old brother Dakota's first communion. She was looking forward to catching up with her siblings and a much-needed dose of normality. Unfortunately, she ended up with the exact opposite.

It was a warm spring afternoon and Dina had arranged a celebration party in their garden. Lindsay had accompanied the family to church but had stopped off on the way home to visit an aunt. Michael was in a more positive mood. Cracking jokes and gesticulating wildly, he was happy keeping his guests entertained. An endless stream of family friends had lavished compliments on the family for Lindsay's recent success. Surely, her doting parents must be very proud. Their comments were well received, but Lindsay was anxious not to detract from her brother's celebrations. It was his day after all. After making her excuses, she quietly snuck out through the back door. She would later kick herself for not staying to keep an eye on her dad.

Dina and Michael were both hunched over the barbeque bickering about what to throw on the grill next. Ali was chasing Dakota around the garden, teasing him for wearing a suit. A car screeched to a halt outside the house and Dina's brother Matt Sullivan stepped out from behind the driving seat. Frowning with intent, he made a beeline directly for Michael.

Earlier that month, following a blazing row with Dina, Michael had called Lindsay and warned her to keep away from her mother's side of the family.

The two had never been friends.

The two men confronted each other on the lawn and a scuffle ensued, with punches flying in all directions. Guests gasped in horror, while children started to cry. Dina screamed at the men, begging them to act like adults and calm down. The fight finally ended when Michael, who was wearing a ring, swung a right hook at Matt's head. The ring ripped through his scalp, causing blood to stream from the gash. Police were called to break up the disturbance, and Matt was taken to hospital for stitches to his head. 'He wound up getting staples in the head,' Michael later said. 'I don't know if it was six or sixteen.'

According to Michael, he had simply defended his family. 'It was my son's communion party. We were having a great time. It was a wonderful day,' he protested to American scandal show *Celebrity Justice*. 'Then he swung at me. I had to defend myself. He threw a garbage bag at me, and I am in a suit. So I pushed him. I did not throw one punch.'

Although Lindsay had missed the actual drama, she was distraught when news of the fight reached her. She was the only family member capable of influencing her father and regretted not being on hand to help out. 'As much as my father tried therapy, I was the only one who could calm him down,' she sighed, discussing her father's temperament with a friend. Tearfully, she pleaded with Michael to control his aggression and enrol in anger-management classes. 'Daddy, I want my family back,' she cried. 'Let's put this back together.'

Michael admits he felt ashamed of himself. The last thing he'd wanted was to hurt his daughter. 'I'm 44 years old and I should know better,' he sighed. 'I studied martial arts for eight years. I know the passive attitude and I didn't use it but I am addressing that – I'm going into anger management.' Speaking of Lindsay's emotional plea, he continued, 'She's a trouper. But she did what she had to.'

Unfortunately for Michael, not everyone involved shared Lindsay's sympathetic viewpoint. Labelling his errant brother-in-law a 'menace of society', Matt Sullivan pressed charges for assault leading to Michael's arrest. His recollection of events was very different to Michael's own. 'I was getting out of a car and he struck me from behind with a shoe then proceeded to beat me once I was bleeding pretty profusely,' Matt told police.

The entire episode was quickly becoming a farce.

Angered by the accusations, Michael threatened to press counter-charges. Lindsay was appalled by the whole affair, which was well documented in the press. The fact that her father had the audacity to speak about the incident on a TV chat show was even more embarrassing. Michael was single-handedly turning the Lohan household into a media circus.

Further trouble came when a business associate claimed Michael had defaulted on a $165,000 (£91,670) loan he'd taken out to start a production company. Michael's finances had been spiralling out of control for quite some time, but he'd so far managed to keep his family out of the picture. Pathetic attempts to protect his children had failed and it looked likely that Lindsay's plush Long Island, New York home would be repossessed. For a man who had once been the most affluent proprietor in his neighbourhood, it was a sad state of affairs.

Dina was furious, but not at all surprised; she always feared things would turn out bad. John Gerard, who had previously filed a lawsuit against the debt, claimed Michael had defaulted on the loan, despite countless promises he would pay back the capital. 'I got [Michael] on the phone, five, six, eight times and he's going to bring the money in,' he claimed. 'Never did pay me back.'

After the initial lawsuit, Michael had signed a settlement agreeing to pay $20,000 (£11,100) immediately and the remaining balance by 2003. But the cash never materialised. After failing to hear anything for nine months, John Gerard took further action.

No longer financially dependent on her father and with a healthy wage packet of her own, Lindsay felt increasingly responsible for her other family members. Dina already received a cut of her income as manager of her daughter's business affairs. Lindsay was now even more determined her father wouldn't get his hands on her money, as she feared he'd squander it all on drink or drugs. Acknowledging that he was completely at fault, Michael attempted to take charge of the situation and promised to pay back the loan. As far as Lindsay and Dina were concerned, however, his empty promises were too few and too late.

Contrary to the assurances he'd given Lindsay, Michael failed to improve his temperament. On countless occasions, the police were called out to settle disputes at the Lohan household. With Dina spending more time away with Lindsay on business trips, the arguments had intensified. Michael was jealous of the relationship that had developed between mother and daughter. Emotionally and financially, he'd been left out of the picture. The press, meanwhile, couldn't get enough of the daily scandals. Every time a new story emerged, they eagerly pounced on fresh morsels of juicy gossip. Perversely, Michael was enjoying the attention he was finally receiving.

His lawyer, Dominic Barbara, would later claim Michael's troubles in fact stemmed from an 'inner turmoil over the dissolution of his family'. Having alienated his next of kin, he now felt abandoned and desperately sought pity. 'The tragedy of Mr Lohan's life at this time is that he feels abandoned by his daughter, Lindsay, and by his wife and children,' said his lawyer in a statement to the press. 'No one's talking to him, and he feels particularly abandoned.'

Michael voiced his concerns to the press. 'All my life I supported them!' he said. 'I took care of them... all of my life. And then, when Lindsay finally hit, I could see it coming... how Dina was starting to mould, get all her friends around her, have her family around her, and start siding with them.'

In June 2004, Michael Lohan was due to appear in court for the charges Matt Sullivan had made against him only a month earlier. Wearing his best suit and a charming smile, Michael hoped to win over the courtroom. Standing to hear a list of accusations read out, he bowed his head with humility. But any attempts to ingratiate himself with the court were useless; the entire hearing dissolved into disarray when Michael was arrested for an entirely different crime. Making a dramatic entrance, police stormed into the room and handcuffed him on the spot. Dina was speechless. The charges read against him involved a dispute over an unpaid hotel bill.

According to management at the upmarket Oheka Castle Hotel, Michael had skipped on a $3,800 bill in April. He had apparently booked several suites for guests and refused to hand over the money, despite the hotel's many attempts to contact him. Michael's lawyer called the arrest a 'cheap shot' and complained that the dramatic display had been completely unnecessary. Afterwards, he told newspapers the incident had simply been down to bad credit. 'As far as I know, Michael arranged to have the bill paid via credit card and, for reasons he was not aware of, the card did not go through. No one contacted him, no one let him know the bill didn't get paid, and, next thing you know, two cops show up at the courthouse.'

Once the commotion had subsided, Michael was released on a $250 bond after being charged with misdemeanour for theft of services.

But the courthouse drama was only just beginning. A hearing was readjourned for the following month. Those weren't the only charges; Michael was also facing prosecution for punching a New York sanitation worker. The incident had occurred in December 2003 when, according to the complaint, Michael lashed out at a binman for blocking his car into a parking space on a Manhattan street. Fuming because 'he had places to go', he was alleged to have then punched the truck driver 'several times about the face with closed fists'.

Aware that Michael Lohan's activities were rapidly attracting a media feeding frenzy, the judge had agreed to combine all three prosecutions into one hearing in a bid to minimise the amount of stress caused to Lindsay. Michael arrived in court looking thoughtful and sombre. His long-suffering mother had chosen to accompany him and lend moral support. Michael's lawyer had warned that the odds were stacked against him; the best he could do was show some remorse.

Becoming anxious, he started to perspire and loosened the collar of his shirt to cool down. But his temperature kept soaring. Suddenly giddy, Michael stood up and prepared to answer assault charges. Feeling a sudden twinge in his chest, he doubled over with pain. Gasping for air, he suddenly collapsed. Having suffered a history of heart problems, Michael was rushed to a nearby medical centre and treated for high blood pressure. He remained there for several days and, once again, the hearing was rescheduled.

For the most part, Lindsay tried to distance herself from the legal wranglings surrounding her father. She was already having difficulty holding herself together and any further emotional involvement could easily cause her to snap. Protective of her daughter's interests, Dina was determined her disastrous marital affairs wouldn't interfere with Lindsay's career. Wherever possible, she tried to shield Lindsay from events and advised her to take no notice of newspaper headlines. Often, Lindsay was totally oblivious to her father's whereabouts. It was easier that way. Even the day before Michael's hearing, Lindsay was unaware he was due in court. When a journalist informed her, she seemed surprised. 'He is?' she said, raising an eyebrow. 'No one tells me. But there's been a lot of stuff going on with him.' When Lindsay heard Michael was in hospital, she was naturally concerned for his health. To her relief, hospital doctors confirmed her father to be in a stable condition.

Not everyone was as sympathetic to her father as Lindsay was. Her grandmother (Dina's mother) blamed Michael for causing her grandchildren distress and tearing the family apart. Ann Sullivan fumed, 'We're all much happier when he's in jail and not around.' She accused, 'He is obsessive possessive – to the point where he doesn't want anyone else being friendly with his wife and children.' In contrast, she praised Lindsay for her strength and patience, claiming the ambitious young actress had found solitude in her successful career. 'It's a Cinderella story,' she mused. 'I think she has a way of talking to God about her problems.'

Reluctant to attribute any of Lindsay's qualities to her father, Ann compared the rising star with her mother. 'She was a very disciplined dancer. I think that's what Lindsay inherited. They have both worked very hard to earn their way in the profession.'

Surrounded by a strong family support network, Lindsay struggled to deal with her father's steady decline. In her darker moments, she would often lay part of the blame at her own door. After all, her profile as a film star had only intensified pressures on the family. 'I feel like sometimes, if I wasn't involved in this, it wouldn't be like that,' she confessed. 'But my dad's a grown man and he's acted very irrationally because of overuse of certain substances. I love him 'cause he's my dad, but I don't respect him as a person. As I got older, I was finally able to say, "Listen, this isn't right."'

With greater distance between herself and Michael, Lindsay could assess the situation more objectively. 'When I think about it, it kind of just registers to me that it was in the papers that my father's going to jail. I think about that and I'm like, wow, that's really hard. People usually don't deal with that in the public eye, for whoever it may be to see.'

But, rather than languishing in self-pity, Lindsay wanted to move on with her life. Often she'd seek solace in her journal. She carried the book around with her everywhere and it contained her innermost thoughts. Often, Dina would warn her not to take it out in public. If ever it fell into the wrong hands, details of Lindsay's personal life could be splashed across the newsstands. Lindsay shrugged off any such suggestions. Carrying the book on her person made her feel complete. Any spare moment she could find would be spent making an entry. She'd even been known to disappear to the ladies' bathroom for extended periods during a party, simply to scribble down a thought that had sprung to mind. 'Whenever I'm really mad or upset about something, I write it down so I don't let it affect me as much, and that really helps.'

Lindsay knew how to handle herself, but she was concerned for her younger brothers and sister. They were still young and impressionable and didn't really understand what was happening to their father. As Michael's misdemeanours became headline news, inevitably the playground taunts followed suit. 'I have three other siblings and it's very hard for them right now – they have no father.'

As for the added media attention, Lindsay had already learned to let the tabloid tittle-tattle wash over her. She knew it came with the territory. It was something she accepted when she first stepped into the limelight. 'I'm a normal person, I have issues, but my life is out there, and I accept it. I don't care if people are going to write about me – they can put it on me. But the reason it upsets me to read about the situation with my dad in the tabloids is because I have three siblings and they have to go to school and hear about it. That hurts me the most, because I feel like a lot of this is my fault.'

In many ways, Lindsay had resigned herself to the fact that her personal life was now being played out in the public arena. In many ways, she mused, it was better the press had something real to write about rather than regurgitating unsubstantiated rumours. She was also tired of keeping secrets and covering up with false smiles. For so long she'd carried the burden of her parents' conflict, while putting on a brave front for the cameras. Lindsay did enough acting in her professional life to carry it on off screen as well. 'It's actually been kind of relaxing, being able to let people know that my family's not perfect,' she sighed. 'I'd rather talk about it and let people know the truth than have people wonder.'

In September 2004, Michael was finally sentenced for his assault on the New York sanitation worker. He pleaded guilty of 'recklessly causing injury to another person'. As part of a rehabilitation process, the Manhattan criminal court judge ordered that he complete an anger-management programme. If he finished the course and remained out of trouble between then and his next court appearance on 9 December, the judge agreed to remove the assault conviction from his record.

Despite any good intentions Michael might have had, everyone knew he would have difficulty keeping his nose out of trouble. For a man who courted drama like a long-lost sweetheart, three months was a long time to stay clean. 'I just want stability for my family,' pleaded Michael as he left the courtroom. 'That's what God wants and everybody wants.' On his way out, he turned to thank an officer whom he credited for saving his life only a month earlier when he'd collapsed of chest pains. The officer had given him on-the-spot treatment for heart problems, including oxygen, aspirin and nitroglycerin pills to lower his blood pressure. More recently, Michael Lohan has been uncharacteristically quiet and reflective. Although now in much better physical health, he knew deep down that no amount of medication could mend a broken heart.

10

DRIVING MISS LOHAN

While Lindsay struggled with personal turmoil, signs indicated that her career path was heading skywards at a supersonic rate. She was now considered one of Hollywood's hottest 'It' girls and was ranked among the highest-paid actresses in the world, pulling in a whopping $7.5 million a movie. While her agents waded through endless scripts and film offers, the demand for Lindsay in the press was equally high. When MTV invited the charismatic teen to host their annual music awards, she became the youngest person ever to take charge of the event. Lindsay had watched the event religiously as a kid, so being involved meant a lot to her. Looking back, she describes it as an unbelievable experience. 'It's weird... I'd see actresses like Jodie Foster and think how much I'd like to do that. Like I used to watch the

MTV Movie Awards and think it would be so cool to go to them. Then, the first time I went to them, I was actually hosting them. It's kind of surreal in a way.'

Having impressed the *Saturday Night Live* crew with her performance in *Mean Girls*, Lindsay was also invited to play host on the prestigious show. She would be the youngest presenter ever in the programme's history. She seemed to be making a habit of breaking these records. Given her natural affinity for comedy, the producers had no qualms about handing over the responsibility. 'I'm really excited,' she gushed. 'I go to New York on Wednesday and then on Sunday I start rehearsing.'

In that time, Lindsay would have to refine her routine and sharpen her skills as a small-screen comedienne. Speaking about the improvised nature of the material, she said, 'They don't come up with anything until that actual week. I've gone to a couple of shows and seen it. It's crazy. It's a whirlwind week.'

Lindsay's performance went down a storm, with critics genuinely impressed by her deft and witty delivery. Never afraid to parody herself, Lindsay even took the opportunity to poke fun at her ongoing rivalry with Hilary Duff in the opening monologue. *SNL* regular Rachel Dratch dressed up as Hilary, singing that the rivalry was 'so yesterday'.

While the American public found her skit hysterical, Hilary was not amused. What was supposed to be a bit of light-hearted fun only served to widen fissures between the rival stars. 'When I heard that Lindsay was going to be on *Saturday Night Live*, I knew she was going to make fun of me,' she told TV show *Access Hollywood*. 'I wasn't honoured. I don't think it's an honour to be made fun of on *Saturday Night Live*.' But, refusing to be drawn into a public argument, Hilary attempted to take the moral high ground. 'I'm not here to talk bad about her like she talks bad about me all the time. I just knew that it was gonna happen.'

Although obviously upset by the incident, Hilary claimed she hadn't been insulted. 'I don't really think she likes me very much,' she shrugged, 'I think it's really mean when they make fun of people. If I ever hosted *Saturday Night Live*, I wouldn't do a skit about her.'

In her defence, Lindsay made a public statement about the TV jibes. 'We didn't do anything derogatory towards her. I'm sorry if she felt offended, but I thought things were cool. Hilary, I don't wanna start anything again!'

Earlier in the year, Lindsay had made a grand gesture towards reconciliation with Hilary on the popular MTV show *TRL*. Presenter Damien Fahey had asked her what one thing she'd like to get out in the open. 'I love you, Hilary Duff!' she blurted. Although intended to raise a smile, there was an element of sincerity to her words. She went on to explain how much she wished the ridiculous rivalry between the pair would end. 'I have no problem with her. Maybe she has a problem with me but I don't think she should.' She went on to compliment Hilary on her new CD and even confessed her little sister Ali was a fan. Over time, rumours about the pair had become increasingly absurd. 'I read recently I had a dartboard of Hilary in my apartment,' laughed Lindsay incredulously. 'Why would I take the time to put up a photo on a dartboard of someone I am cool with? It's just silly stuff.'

But the controversy wasn't about to die down just yet. Eyebrows were raised about the song 'Haters' on Hilary's second album. Had the following lyrics been written about anyone in particular? 'You're queen of superficiality, keep your lies out of my reality... You say your boyfriend's sweet and kind, but you've still got your eyes on mine.'

But Hilary was quick to slam reports, claiming tabloid gossips had misconstrued her words. 'They're just rumours,' she sighed, now fed up with the whole debacle. 'I would never write a song about her. I don't know her!'

What had started out as a teenage tiff over a boy had become full-blown rivalry. Both parties felt it was time to draw a close to any further wicked whispers. 'This whole thing is like so blown out of proportion,' continued Lindsay. 'I honestly don't know her. Of course, I've met her before, but I don't know her and I'm kind of done with it.'

However, the pair weren't about to start exchanging pleasantries just yet. More problems arose when Hilary's new boyfriend, Joel Madden, of rock boy band Good Charlotte, refused to give Lindsay's eight-year-old brother Cody an autograph. The tabloids seized on the opportunity to inflame the dying rivalry, causing tensions to rise once again. Apparently, Joel had refused to entertain Cody and his friend's request backstage at the Jingle Ball Radio Festival in New York. While Lindsay's publicist refused to comment on the incident, a Good Charlotte spokesperson claimed it had never even taken place.

Regardless of who was really to blame in the ongoing disagreement, Lindsay found herself in hot water with mental-health watchdogs after branding Hilary 'retarded' in interviews. The US-based ARC organisation was outraged and complained in a public statement, 'There are few more deeply wounding words than these, which are painful reminders that people with disabilities are still not fully welcome in our society.'

Lindsay's publicist Leslie Sloane Zelnik responded on her behalf, claiming Lindsay had never intended to upset anyone. 'It wasn't meant to offend anyone – it was used as slang,' she explained. 'She'll be more cautious and conscious in the future.'

Although Lindsay was sincerely sorry she'd upset anyone, she would later joke to journalists, 'I'd better watch my language!'

As both girls' careers rocketed skywards, it was inevitable that their paths would cross more frequently. They shared the same friends, fans and, often, red carpet. Admittedly, they'd once shared the same boy but, with new beaus in tow, the argument now seemed childishly absurd. Lindsay was tired of reading the same old headlines and needed to move on. If she wanted to be taken seriously as an adult actress, playground disputes such as these would have to end. Nor was it a good example to set Lindsay's younger fans, who looked up to her as a role model.

Lindsay made one last-ditch attempt at reconciliation. Picking up her sparkling pink mobile phone, she tentatively dialled Hilary's home number. 'Hello?' she said, unaware of who had actually picked up at the other end. Feeling slightly nervous, she blurted out, 'Do you want to hang out?'

Unfortunately, Hilary was out shopping with friends, and her sister had picked up the phone. Unsure of what to do, she simply hung up on Lindsay. Initially furious, Lindsay was still glad to have made the gesture. If Hilary wanted it, the olive branch was there for the taking. 'It was like, literally,

four years ago when that happened, we were 14...
15... we liked a boy, it was like a crush,' shrugged
Lindsay. 'Besides, I don't like having enemies... and
there's the saying, keep your friends close but your
enemies closer.'

Unfortunately, Lindsay's enemies would end up
causing her far less heartache than her so-called
friends. While most pals treated Lindsay no differently,
inevitably some tried to take advantage of her fame.
Already, she'd received calls out of the blue from 'long-
lost pals' who suddenly wanted to meet up and hang
out. But Lindsay wasn't stupid. She knew the people
she could trust – or at least she thought she did.

In August 2004, Lindsay experienced her first
fender bender. Having recently acquired her licence,
Lindsay had treated herself to a BMW convertible
with a personalised number plate spelling
ILLEGALL. 'My parents are nervous,' she joked, 'it's
a really fast car and they wanted me to get a truck.'

But, rather than let her parents fork out for a car,
Lindsay took it upon herself to buy a second-hand
vehicle. She even put a new engine in. While driving
along Laurel Canyon Boulevard on a sunny August
afternoon, Lindsay suffered an unfortunate collision
with another car. Visibly shaken, she leaped from her
vehicle to examine the damage. Predictably, the
paparazzi were not far behind and pictures of the star
in baseball cap and flip-flops would appear in the

papers the following day. The actual damage caused was minimal, although the owners of the other vehicle would later sue Lindsay for personal injury. As if she needed any more contact with the law courts!

But, while Lindsay was left unscathed, her squeaky-clean Disney reputation was left virtually in tatters. The following week, an account of the incident appeared in gossip bible *US Weekly* suggesting that the accident had been caused by negligent driving after a particularly late night. Lindsay was horrified. She was currently up for a starring role in a Disney remake of cult '80s flick *Herbie*. Lindsay was set to play a young girl obsessed by motor racing, so the allegations couldn't have come at a worse time. 'I almost didn't get the part because of that story!' she later complained. 'They [Disney] thought I was trouble.'

Lindsay was even further dismayed to discover the source of the story had been a close friend. 'Someone I thought was my friend reported it to *US Weekly* and made up all these lies about what I did. The story that came out made it seem like I'd been out partying and got into an accident. The other guy hit me! I was going to a meeting at three in the afternoon and they made it seem like it was three in the morning.' Needless to say, when Lindsay finally tracked down the mole they were instantly erased from her Blackberry.

Betrayed at such close quarters, Lindsay began to wonder whom she could really trust. 'I was going through the phase of wanting to be with my family more,' she recalls. Uncertain of her new surroundings, she began to wonder if she actually had any friends. If she needed someone, would they be there in a flash just like they had been in New York?

Lindsay also grew concerned about photographers trailing her car. Desperate to get a shot of the star, they would go to any lengths to track her down. She'd already caused a near emergency by trying to shake off paparazzi during a car chase. 'I jumped to the police station,' she says, recalling the story in adrenalin-fuelled detail. 'But I didn't realise that the spot that I pulled into was this emergency spot. So I pulled into this spot and sirens started going off in the police station. All of these voices start saying you've to push the button to say what the emergency is; they probably thought that somebody was dying and, like, bleeding to death. So I run out of the car and what do the paparazzi do? They stop and start taking pictures of me talking to a cop in front of a police station.' Losing her composure for a moment and forgetting her promises to the ARC mental-health group, she sighed, 'It's so retarded.'

Lindsay was in too high a demand for any of the allegations really to matter. Disney were more than happy with Lindsay and she landed her role in *Herbie:*

Fully Loaded. When her agents called with news of the deal, she couldn't believe the salary she was being offered. A whopping $7.5 million was more than the 18-year-old could imagine and it put her in a super league with actresses like Kirsten Dunst. Lindsay would star as Maggie Peyton, a girl desperate to race cars, despite the disapproval of her stock-car driver father, Ray (played by Michael Keaton). As the film plays out, Lindsay's character develops a relationship with a VW Beetle that can think for itself.

Lindsay had only one hesitation about accepting the part – she was concerned that people might think she was incapable of carrying an original script. 'I'm thinking about it now and it's kind of funny that I've done all these Disney remakes,' she giggled. 'But I'm a big fan of older movies, so it's nice to be the one to remake those and bring them back.'

Determined to make the character of Maggie her own, Lindsay refused to watch 1968's *The Love Bug*, the original Herbie film. 'I didn't watch the original,' she said, adding that the producers had advised her against it. 'It's the same storyline, but it's very different from this one. You have to update it for the times. It frightens me to watch the originals [of my movies] sometimes.'

Initially, Lindsay wondered how on earth she would talk to a car convincingly. 'I think, whenever someone gets their car, it becomes their baby,' she mused on the role. 'In the movie, you form a bond with this car and you feel for it. He's the underdog and everyone always roots for the underdog! At first, I thought it was silly, but I wanted to bring the relationship to life and I wanted people to see how cute Herbie can be... kinda like a pet!'

Her director, Angela Robinson, commended her performance. 'It's an incredibly difficult acting challenge to actually act with a car,' she admitted. 'The reason the movie is successful is that you believe she has a relationship with Herbie, which she just does so effortlessly.'

The film also required Lindsay to perform some stunts behind the wheel. No stranger to slamming her foot on the accelerator in car chases, she joked that the training would probably come in useful! 'I have a lead foot!' she laughed. 'There's a huge adrenalin rush when you're driving fast in cars. But it's kinda dangerous,' she hastened to add. 'It's nice to drive fast, but I don't encourage it.'

Lindsay did admit that manoeuvring skills she'd learned on set had helped her as a driver. Another new skill Lindsay had to lock down for her role was skateboarding. Initially, she'd begged the director to rewrite the part, fearing it was too dangerous. She had never set foot on a skateboard in her life. But Angela insisted she give it a go, suggesting that Lindsay needed to push herself harder, instead of giving up at the first hurdle. Angela hoped that a sense of achievement would give her young star a rush of confidence. At first, Lindsay couldn't get the hang of it and kept falling over in fits of laughter. But, after a few attempts, she nailed it, thus adding a further string to her already bristling bow.

On set, Lindsay impressed her co-stars with a standard she'd already set with previous films. She recalls one particular scene involving a fight with Michael Keaton, which she describes as her favourite. 'It's something different and something new,' she said at the time. 'It's refreshing to do that, just because it brings out other emotions.'

Michael Keaton admiringly went on to describe his co-star as 'a young lady who's come a long way quickly and is going to go even further'. Breckin Meyer, who plays her brother in the film, was equally wowed by Lindsay's ability to delight the camera. 'She just has it… she's got that kind of spark where you just want to watch her. She's charismatic and talented, that's kinda it.' He was also amazed by Lindsay's incredible recall ability. 'She has this photographic memory, which ticks me off as an actor. She learns her lines like that,' he complained, snapping his fingers by way of demonstration. 'It drives you insane.'

Lindsay's ability to learn her lines at the drop of a hat had been commented on before. 'I have this weird thing, since I was a kid – I think that's how I got through *Parent Trap* – and I don't even understand it,' she confesses. 'My dad's the same way... he just looks at something and he kind of remembers it right away. I look at the lines and I can do the scene. It's very strange.'

During breaks between filming, Lindsay would hang out with her co-stars or watch horror movies in her trailer. Her good friend Kendra was working on an electronic press kit for the film and her mum would often drop by to spend time with her daughter. The women would gossip about news stories, fashion and mutual friends. Lindsay's co-stars also played several practical jokes on her. 'They tortured me!' she joked to one interviewer.

Lindsay remembered the occasion well. The crew had travelled to Acton, California to film some of the car-race scenes. Miles from any civilisation, they'd set up camp in the middle of the desert. The scorching sun had been beating down on the cast all day, but as soon as night fell the temperature dropped significantly. Fortunately, Lindsay had been in the shade all day, shooting scenes in a dilapidated barn. Inside the building, windows were hanging from broken hinges and it was unlikely any living soul had passed through there in years. The whole place instantly gave Lindsay the creeps; it reminded her of the house in *Texas Chainsaw Massacre*. Breckin even cracked a joke about bloodstains on the outer walls, which turned out to be nothing more than rust.

As a cold wind whistled through the draughty rafters, Lindsay shuddered and retreated to her trailer. Perhaps she wouldn't be watching any horror movies tonight! As the crew switched out their lights for the night, an eerie silence fell. Lindsay pulled herself into bed and reached over to set her alarm clock. Suddenly, everything went pitch black. Lindsay flicked the light switch, but nothing happened. She'd totally lost power. Then, from outside, she heard a strange sucking noise. Her trailer started to shake and, before she could investigate the source of any activity further, she lost her balance and toppled to the ground. For a split-second she was totally freaked out, but muffled voices outside instantly gave the game away – her co-stars were setting her up. 'They put a vacuum on outside that sounded like a chainsaw,' explained Lindsay. 'Then they jumped on the trailer and shook it. Breckin was underneath the trailer, and Justin [Long] was on top of it!' Fortunately for her pals, Lindsay joined in the joke. 'I was pretty good about it,' she laughed.

Breckin had a way of lifting Lindsay's spirits and she loved to be around him on set. Whenever she was feeling tired, he always managed to raise a smile. Lindsay couldn't help but associate him with the goofy character he'd played in *Clueless*. 'Breckin is hysterical,' squealed Lindsay. 'He's just genuinely a guy who doesn't try to be funny at all but he just is. We goof around a lot... we have a lot of fun.' But after his failed chainsaw gag, Breckin was even more determined to catch Lindsay out. 'I don't know where they found it, but they found this huge stuffed spider,' recalls Lindsay, still amused by the childish prank. 'It looked so realistic, and he came out of the car and slid out and it was on top of him and I freaked out and screamed and everything!'

While filming, Lindsay also formed a valuable friendship with Matt Dillon. Keen to learn from professionals in the field, she observed his acting technique and took on board some useful tips. 'When I'm on set, I'm all over the place thinking about 20 different things,' she confessed. 'I'll be on the cell phone talking to my friend or my mom until we roll and then I'll jump back on the phone. Matt Dillon has been a good teacher; when he's on the set, he is always focused and intense. I want to be more like that.'

Lindsay would be the first to admit that most of the characters she'd played thus far had never demanded that degree of emotional involvement. But it was something she intended to investigate further. Whenever a particularly complicated scene did come up, she would retreat to her trailer for a quiet period of reflection. Matt Dillon warmed to Lindsay after drawing similarities with himself as a young actor. 'Lindsay is really talented,' he told reporters. 'I identify with her because I was at that age where I was under a certain scrutiny as she is. I've been high-tailed by the paparazzi over the years but I think her experience is much more intense.'

The physical demands of filming *Herbie* were unlike anything Lindsay had experienced before. Alongside the tricky stunt work, she also had to shoot scenes in the desert regions of Acton and Fontana, wearing full NASCAR racing suits in temperatures of up to 120°C. 'Thank God, we got to take the lining out of ours,' says Lindsay shaking her head. 'We were sweating to death.'

The young star's daily work schedule was also more gruelling than ever before. Having turned 18, any work restrictions on the length of her workdays no longer applied. Lindsay's workload had subsequently increased at an alarming rate. She was turning into a workaholic, but at least her only vice was work. During *Herbie*'s 70-day shoot, she was due on set at 4.30am each morning and often wouldn't return home until two in the morning. 'I'd literally sleep, and then sleep in the car for an hour,' she shudders. On several occasions, she'd wake up unable to face another day of work but, aware of her professional commitments, she soldiered on. 'Work's a lot like going to school,' she mused. 'You wake up and you go, "How can I fake being sick?" But I can't do that, because I have obligations to so many people.'

Lindsay had only just moved in with Wilmer, but the couple were barely spending any time together. 'I don't think anybody realises the amount of work she does,' said director Angela Robinson at the time. 'On her one day off, she did three interviews and then a photo shoot and a wardrobe change for her next movie. Everybody says, "She's 18, she'll be fine," but she's working way harder than anybody should.'

Another disaster struck when Lindsay took some time off to record an MTV diary in Cancun. On one of her days off, the sun-hungry star leaped at an opportunity to catch some rays. She'd already developed a taste for tanning, with visits to salon Mystic Tan, so she wasn't about to miss out on the real thing. Irresponsibly, she forgot to apply any suntan lotion. Tired from her heavy workload, she drifted off to sleep.

When she awoke a couple of hours later, she was in agony. She looked down at her legs to discover they were blistering and red. In a panic, Lindsay called for her assistant, who immediately drove her to Casualty. Once in hospital, she was treated for second-degree burns. 'I lay out in the sun under an umbrella,' she later recounted. 'I fell asleep but wasn't too worried because I knew I was covered, but the sun shifted and it started hitting me. So, when I woke up, I could barely move. I got second-degree burns on my stomach and legs and first-degree burns on my face. It was terrible.'

Distraught, she phoned up Dina in tears. 'I was hysterical – crying and bawling, 'cause my mom was in New York with all my family. And I was on the phone crying, "I need you, Mom."'

Adding to her pressures, Lindsay was also in the process of recording her début album, *Speak*. Several months earlier, in July, she'd secured a deal with Casablanca Records. The label belonged to Mariah Carey's ex-husband Tommy Mottola, who'd nurtured the world-famous singer's early career. He recognised a similar star quality in Lindsay. 'Her whole lifestyle and attitude encompass everything teenagers are going through,' he enthused. 'And. if you want to have a huge, successful album, that's really the market you want… I'm thrilled we have her. I think she's the next big star on the horizon.'

In fact, the music mogul was so pleased with his new signing that he went out and bought her a giant picture of her heroine Marilyn Monroe. Lindsay was extremely touched by the gesture. Tommy was desperate for Lindsay to release material. Dina, with a mother's concern, worried that the time frame was unrealistic. Humorously, Lindsay labelled herself a glutton for punishment. 'I know! I'm crazy. I like to torture myself.' But the volume of work she'd unwittingly taken on was not a joke.

Lindsay rushed her album, recording almost every song in her trailer on the set of *Herbie*. 'I was literally running from set, in between set-ups, and singing,' she shudders. But the impracticalities of recording next to the Californian Speedway became too great. 'I can't record the album in a trailer, in a movie set, because we're hearing the cars driving around on the record!' Exhausted from a day's work, Lindsay would head straight into the studio, often finishing at 2.30am. She would even do some recording in her bedroom at home.

Inevitably, Lindsay became tired and irritable on set. 'Can we shoot this shit already?' she'd bark, her voice hoarse from smoking too many cigarettes. Sitting quietly in a corner, she'd recite a Peter Piper tongue twister to keep her mouth and lips warmed up in preparation for a scene. A make-up artist would attempt to style her hair in a particular way, only for Lindsay to grumble before quickly apologising. Some reports suggested Lindsay was barely even on set. Her frequent absences were delaying filming and proving to be extremely costly for the studio. Reasons would range from stomach cramps to headaches, but they were in truth manifestations of exhaustion.

Once again, the press were fixated by Lindsay's

breasts. But now they had a different angle. Tired of peddling stories about enhancement, they'd now moved on to reduction. Lindsay couldn't keep up. Several papers ran a story claiming that Disney bosses had spent an extortionate amount of money in post-production to have Lindsay's womanly figure digitally reduced. One report suggested that the cost of reducing Lindsay's chest by two cup sizes and raising the revealing necklines on her T-shirts had amounted to over $1 million.

Lindsay laughed off any claims as completely absurd. 'Goodness gracious! To go through every scene? Do you know how much money that would cost? That is so silly. I don't know what I've done to deserve people saying things like that about me.'

More stories involving cosmetic surgery would erupt when Lindsay was accused of having her lips pumped with collagen. 'That's insane!' fumed Lindsay. 'I just use Lip Venom [gloss] – it's the best!'

One magazine had invited a plastic surgeon to analyse pictures of Lindsay. 'There's too much swelling,' he reported. 'I don't think you can achieve that kind of affect with Lip Venom.' Lindsay gave up – was there any part of her body she could still claim to be her own?

Perhaps if Disney could digitally clone another Lindsay Lohan, their young star would have time to sit down and catch her breath. As it was, her energy levels were running dangerously low. The cracks were already starting to appear. The last few months were finally catching up with Lindsay and she was burning out fast. Very soon, the young actress would reach breaking point. Sadly, no one saw it coming.

11

GIMME A BREAK!

Although she had convinced plenty of people to think otherwise, deep down Lindsay was still a young girl. Despite her commitment and ambition, there were physical limits to what she could achieve. The emotional strains were becoming more and more apparent. Soon, the pressures would manifest themselves physically.

Lindsay's health problems began in early October 2004, when she was rushed to the dentist after her tooth fell out on set. As they were wrapping up a day's filming, she felt a crack and a sudden shooting pain in the back of her mouth. 'Half my tooth fell out in the back of my mouth!' she later complained. 'I've been avoiding the dentist and I've gotta go after I leave the set.' That was just the beginning.

Subsequently, Lindsay was earning herself a

reputation among the film crew for being accident-prone. While filming a music video for 'First', to be featured on the *Herbie* soundtrack, a car ran over her foot and she twisted her ankle. Due to time restrictions, the video had been recorded in a stressful and frantic hurry. Unhappy with the early shots, director Jake Nava (also responsible for Lindsay's later 'Rumors' video) had pushed for an extra day of shooting.

Tired and frustrated through exhaustion at the time, Lindsay was delighted with the end product. '[I'm] really happy with it,' said Lindsay, after seeing the video for the first time. 'Jake did an amazing job and we had a great team there.'

In the video, Lindsay rocks out on a chequerboard stage, while flashy race cars speed past her. 'We actually got the race cars from *2 Fast 2 Furious*,' she said. 'There's a lot of racing going on and there's a secret behind the [plot], because Herbie comes out in the middle of the video and ends up winning the race.' At the end of the video, Lindsay reveals herself to be the leather-clad babe behind the wheel.

As Lindsay's health slowly deteriorated, toothaches and a twisted ankle would soon be the least of her problems. One day, she felt much worse than usual. Her head was throbbing with stabbing pains. It felt as if someone was driving a knife right through her skull. The doctor had given her some medicine, but on this occasion it was having little effect. She could barely focus her eyes on the script for that day. Already late on set, she struggled to pull herself together. But it was no use; huddled in the corner, she couldn't leave her trailer. 'I started to get really bad head pains, to the point where I was shaking,' she says. 'I got a fever of 102.'

The film crew strongly advised Lindsay to go to hospital immediately, but she stubbornly refused. Instead, she went back to Wilmer's house and lay down on the bed. She tried to sleep, but kept waking up with shooting head pains. Later, when regaling the episode to *Vanity Fair*, she claims she'd never screamed so loudly. 'I was screaming, throwing things, because the pains were so intense in my head, like someone was stabbing me in the head.'

Distressed and confused, Wilmer didn't know what to do. He tried to take care of Lindsay, but she proceeded to scream at him even more.

In the end, she agreed to see a doctor and he sent her straight to hospital. Dina rushed to her daughter's side. She knew Lindsay had been working hard and feared something like this might happen. Doctors told Lindsay her liver had swollen, she had a kidney infection and the production of white blood cells had been accelerated. 'I love how I say it like that,' she laughs after the event. 'I don't know what it means, but it's not good.'

Although the cause of Lindsay's symptoms remained unclear, she was certainly suffering from some kind of exhaustion. Concerned, nurses hooked her up to an IV unit and gave her shots of morphine every two hours to numb the head pains. Dina called the studio to let them know Lindsay would be out of action for at least the next few days. All of her promotional commitments were postponed. Unable to protest, Lindsay had to accept that she needed a rest.

Over the following week, Lindsay's condition seemed to get worse. When close family friend Jesse Schulman arrived to visit from New York, she was distraught to find a frail-looking wisp of a girl who barely resembled the bubbly teen she remembered from home. Lindsay had lost her hair extensions and the fake glow she'd built up from multiple trips to the tanning salon. Unable to eat, she'd also lost an alarming 15 pounds. Shocked by the sight confronting her, Jesse burst into tears and had to leave the room. 'I was really, really white, and I got really, really pale and my hair was really short,' Lindsay later recalled. She went on to describe herself as 'a ghost, like, so tiny and frail-looking'. Lindsay became so weak it was impossible to leave her bed without a walker. 'My legs were so numb... I had a walker to get to the bathroom and back. My body didn't even have enough strength to take a shower.'

In hindsight, Lindsay realised something had to

happen. Deep down, she was secretly relieved her health had intervened and forced her to take the period of rest. Intensive hours on the set of *Herbie*, coupled with the pressures of recording a début album, had stretched the young teen to her physical limits. In one particularly extreme instance, she worked 24 hours straight through. 'When I shot my video, I did a 24-hour day and I was meant to be on set the next morning for filming and I physically couldn't go. There was an impending lawsuit because I was supposed to be there but I couldn't do it.'

Ambitious and desperate to succeed, she had been too frightened to admit something was wrong. Teetering on the brink of a breakdown, it didn't require much to topple her over the edge. 'It was all too much and I couldn't handle it,' she admitted. 'I was overtired and working myself to death. When you're young, you think you can just keep going and going. The hardest thing in this business is to say "No", because so many people want you to say "Yes... yes... yes". I just wanted to make everyone happy, but it gets difficult.'

Speaking about her attempts to juggle two careers at the same time, she said, 'It's nice to be able to have the options to explore the fields that you want to and also to encourage other people to do that. But it gets difficult.'

Lindsay remained in hospital for five days. The

crew shut down on the shoot of *Herbie* and she was left alone to rest. 'I couldn't work. No one could bother me. I could just relax,' she said with a degree of relief. Lindsay started to regard her hospital stay as a vacation; in fact, she even started to enjoy it. 'I know that sounds so sick,' she laughed. 'I watched loads of soap operas!'

It was also the cry for help she'd hitherto felt unable to vocalise. 'I didn't want to complain,' she protested. 'But that was my way to complain, to actually let everyone know – guys, I can only handle so much.'

Lindsay was blissfully unaware that her health had become a topic of frantic concern in the outside world. Whispers about the cause of her illness were flying around film studios. Gossip columnists were grinding the rumour mill and had drawn a link between Lindsay's sudden illness and her 'lavish' party lifestyle. The tabloids caught a whiff of scandal and even hinted that drugs might be involved. When Lindsay found out, she was appalled and would later appear on TV to reassure fans that she'd learned her lesson and was back on track.

When interviewers quizzed her about the likely cause of her breakdown, she remained vague but listed several possible ailments. 'I was really overworked and really tired... had a kidney infection... stress... wasn't eating right... wasn't getting enough sleep... I had an asthma attack... had a cold... a form of mononucleosis... I was really sick... I was really scared.'

Lindsay did confess her party lifestyle probably hadn't helped the situation. 'I was just working, working, working, and tired, and going out with my friends in the wrong way when I should have been resting. I wasn't taking time to stay at home and relax. I felt like I was missing out on something. Los Angeles does that to you. When you hear everyone is going out you think, "Oh, what if something happens and I'm not out?" But, on the advice of her doctors and close family members, Lindsay had agreed to redress her lifestyle and take better care of herself. 'I have to take the time to focus on what's best for me, and surround myself with those people who are going to be honest and supportive.'

News of Lindsay's hospital visit soon reached her father. While the rest of the world was clamouring for gossip on the cause of her condition, Michael Lohan was simply struggling to see his daughter. Days after he'd agreed to enrol in anger-management classes to improve his temperament, Michael had been involved in yet another fracas with his estranged wife. The incident resulted in both parties filing restraining orders to keep the other at least 100 yards away. Michael claimed Dina had tried to run him over, while Dina claimed she was the victim of a potential hit-and-run.

Michael later recounted his version of events to the *New York Post*. Allegedly passing through the area, Michael caught sight of Dina leaving her office. He followed her to a restaurant in a bid to 'talk to her about the kids', but she refused to stop and listen. He entered the restaurant and instructed the maître d' not to let her drink, because she was driving. He claims to have called her later that afternoon to find she was 'sloshed'. Fearing the children were in her company, he called the police. Worried they wouldn't take appropriate action, he drove to Dina's Long Island home and pulled into the driveway behind her as she arrived. 'She tried to jump the kerb and nearly ran me over,' he claimed to the paper.

He went on to describe how Dina's assistant, Ann Occhupinti, leaped out of the vehicle, demanding, 'You want a piece of me?' 'She's 200-plus pounds and she's bigger than me, so I backed away.'

But by the time Nassau County Police arrived to breathalyse Dina, Michael claims she had retreated into hiding at her mother's house. 'She was hiding from police,' he said. 'It's an open case that's been investigated,' Detective Robert Pescitelli was quoted as saying. Nevertheless, it was enough for a judge to slap a restraining order on Michael, denying him any contact with Dina.

Determined to see his sick daughter, Michael

gleaned enough information from newspaper reports to ascertain that Lindsay was staying at the Cedars-Sinai Medical Center. But, on arrival at the hospital, he had trouble in tracking her down; Lindsay had registered under an alias. In addition, she had two security guards posted outside her door.

Pleading with receptionists, Michael attempted to gain entry on two different occasions. But Dina had requested that he leave the family alone. 'I've been here twice and I just want to know that Lindsay is OK,' he complained. 'My wife promised me she won't keep me from my kids. Evidently, not so.' Michael went on to blame Dina for ruining his relationship with the kids. 'It's horrible that there's been such a wall put up around her, when Lindsay and I had an amazing relationship all of our life until this happened. She's being torn up. It's not fair to her or my other children to be put in the middle like this; it's a horrible thing.'

Lindsay was informed that her father had attempted to make contact. She'd not seen him since August when she was dining at the LA restaurant Koi with Paris Hilton and Wilmer. After hearing his daughter was at the restaurant, Michael had turned up unexpectedly. Keen not to create a scene, Lindsay politely said hello before asking him to leave. Michael would later describe the encounter as a happy reunion. According to his version of events, he told Lindsay, 'I've wanted nothing to do with your career other than to see you happy. You mother can have all the fame and glory. I just want to be your best friend.' He said Lindsay responded, 'You've always been my best friend. I just don't want any more of this arguing.'

Deep down, Lindsay wanted to see her father, but she knew that, given the current situation, a family reunion would be inappropriate. 'I have to be honest... I would have liked to have seen him,' she later confessed. 'But my mother was there and my brothers and sister were there and they were scared.'

Michael had the option of simply walking away, but it was not his way. Consumed by a mixture of anger and desperation, he instead turned to the press. Despite numerous reports to the contrary, including the occasion he passed out in Manhattan strip club Scores, Michael insisted, 'I don't have a drink problem.' (The latter incident was apparently a misunderstanding, which occurred after Michael's prescription medication mixed badly with a couple of 'innocent drinks'.) Instead, he argued, certain people were trying to undermine his reputation and destroy his relationship with Lindsay. To his mind, there had never been a problem until the rest of the world had stepped in.

Paradoxically, he continued to court the public's attention. He credited these 'lowlifes' as the cause of his family's problems. 'Her friends are parasites and I said so, so they scorn me. They are trying to put a wedge between me and my daughter,' he told New York gossip column *Page Six*. 'We love each other. But the people around her are lowlifes. It's all "dese", "dem" or "dose". I have tapes you won't believe, and I'll release them at the proper time.'

Michael believed he was the victim of a calculated campaign to destroy his relationship with Lindsay through misrepresentation in the press. He believed that, once certain obstacles had been removed, Lindsay would come running back to her father. 'I have made enemies with them, and now they all want me out, because, if I'm back in the picture, they're going to be gone. Bottom line. And they know it.'

So far, Lindsay had tried to remain impartial to her parents' disagreements. But, when Michael's attacks were aimed directly at her, she could no longer keep quiet. Responding to press speculation, he insinuated that his daughter's hospital stay might have been drug related. 'I've heard the rumours and I won't condone drinking and drugs,' he told gossip rag *US Weekly*. His comments further inflamed an already delicate situation. Lindsay was distraught. She was having enough trouble living down her 'party-girl' reputation, without her father adding fuel to the fire. To make matters worse, Michael made several disapproving remarks about Lindsay's boyfriend

Wilmer. He believed Lindsay's older boyfriend was a substitute for a 'father figure'. He complained, 'How can she look to a 24-year-old guy with no life experience?'

Infuriated by her father's persistence in playing out personal dramas in the press, Lindsay called up an LA radio station to say a few words of her own. Responding to reports that her party lifestyle was affecting her acting career, she screamed, 'That's not true. It's so upsetting.' As for her father, she continued, 'It sucks so much. He's my father and I love him to death but he's not acting rationally right now.' When Sugar Ray singer Mark McGrath (who was presenting the show) intervened to offer his support, Lindsay snapped back wildly, 'I don't need support... this is bullshit.'

While allegations in the press had incensed Lindsay, it was her father's comments that cut the deepest. To hear a member of her own family suggest she'd been involved with drugs upset her immensely. 'It angers me to see that my own father would stoop to such a level,' she sadly admitted to TV show *Access Hollywood*. 'I have tried to keep quiet long enough. Unfortunately, my father has continued to move forward with his actions as a cry for attention. I have been informed that he has started false allegations regarding myself and the cause of my illness.'

On hearing her response, Michael later retracted his comments saying, 'I never said that… never even insinuated it.'

For the first time, Dina publicly admitted her daughter had been affected by Michael's actions. 'It's hurt her deeply, and you don't want to deal with that at 18,' she said.

When Lindsay was finally discharged from hospital, she stepped into a media whirlwind. Elbowing each other for a clear line of sight, a barrage of photographers had gathered outside. Much stronger now, Lindsay held her head high and smiled confidently. She'd dressed up specially, keen to show the world she was back on top form. Lindsay recalled the outfit clearly. 'It was moccasin boots before anyone wore them… these black little leggings… and this Anna Molinari low-cut, pink-with-hearts shirt.'

When Lindsay opened the papers the following morning, her face fell. Fortunately on this occasion, salacious gossip wasn't the cause; the tabloids simply hadn't used her pictures. 'The paparazzi went crazy on her. But they didn't use one of the pictures!' complained her pal Jesse. 'I was so mad because I wanted people to see this cute outfit she'd put together.'

Tongue firmly in cheek, Lindsay would later argue, 'Whenever I wear my best outfits, there's no paparazzi to be seen.' Her sense of humour already on display, Lindsay was clearly on the mend.

Feeling stronger and more confident, Lindsay was now ready to return to work. Her first commitment was a cameo appearance alongside her boyfriend in TV comedy *That '70s Show*. Filming had been postponed following Lindsay's sudden sickness. She played a girl call Danielle who falls in love with Wilmer's character Fez after meeting him in a hair salon.

During shooting, Lindsay befriended co-star Ashton Kutcher's future wife Demi Moore. She introduced Lindsay to the cult philosophy Kabbalah, and suggested it might provide a solution to her recent problems. 'I did start to look into the whole Kabbalah thing a while ago, just because my mom was like, "Maybe you should try it!"' she later admitted. 'It kind of interested me, because they talk about ego and stuff. But I don't really have an ego. I mean, everybody does in a way. When you're in a relationship, you have an ego. Especially if the other person is in the business.'

To all intents and purposes, it seemed to the outside world that Lindsay's life might be back on track. Her health issues had been addressed and she appeared to have settled down with a stable boyfriend. But, just days later, that illusion appeared to shatter when reports were leaked that Lindsay and Wilmer had split up. While Lindsay's people declined to comment, a spokeswoman for Wilmer confirmed that, for once, there was truth to the rumour. Wilmer had been a solid rock of support to Lindsay. 'He's been there for me with all this family shit going on,' she told reporters. Without him, there was a chance she could crumble. The split was yet another blow to the already fragile star. Was Lindsay Lohan about to go under?

12

YOUNG, FREE...
AND SINGLE

The second half of 2004 had been a difficult period for Lindsay Lohan. Anyone involved in her close circle inevitably became swept up in the whirlwind of events that seemed to accompany her lifestyle. After Dina, Wilmer was the first person Lindsay would turn to in her times of need. Although they had only been publicly dating since Lindsay's 18th birthday, the couple had been practically living together for the last nine months. Increasingly consumed by her work, Lindsay would often bring her problems home with her. Upbeat and smiling in the public eye, by the time Lindsay reached Wilmer she was often tired and miserable. Everyone was desperate for a piece of Lindsay Lohan, and her boyfriend often had to settle for leftovers.

When the relationship between her parents started

to collapse publicly, Lindsay relied heavily on Wilmer for support. Lonely and insecure, she wanted to be with him 'every five seconds'. Looking back, she says, there was no one else to turn to. Even though Wilmer was six years her senior, there was still only so much a 24-year-old could handle. The couple were seen quarrelling in several clubs and frequent arguments were overheard from Lindsay's trailer on the *Herbie* set. 'They would argue, and then Lindsay would be in her trailer crying for hours,' said a set hand.

Gossip columnists would later suggest that Wilmer had decided to end the relationship weeks before Lindsay went into hospital; he was simply being a gentleman and standing by the ailing star while she recuperated. Dina dismissed the arguments as teething problems and described any disagreements as the tiffs young lovers naturally experience. But Lindsay already knew the relationship was running into problems. 'I'm ruining this relationship with this guy that I think is my first love,' she says in retrospect. 'I'm ruining it because I'm taking everything out on him.'

Things came to a head during a cover photo shoot for *Jane* magazine. According to reports, Lindsay became upset when Wilmer phoned up to say he couldn't collect her from the photographic studio. Afterwards, her publicist refuted the claims saying, 'Lindsay is a professional and the shoot was fine.' It was obvious Lindsay's romance was on the rocks.

Although she refused to discuss details in the press, Lindsay later admitted it was Wilmer who had chosen to end the relationship. She was heartbroken. When quizzed on the cause of the break-up, she appeared confused. 'We dated for nine months. We were, like, living with each other. It was serious! I don't really know why we broke up. I knew I was going to have to travel a lot and I was willing to actually not do my movies and stay with him. And now I'm just kind of left with nothing, like, "I just gave you all my life and said I would not do this any more for you, and now you've left me in the dust."'

Lindsay had pledged her whole life to Wilmer, even hinting at plans of future marriage. Lindsay had also made statements in the press about wanting to be a young mum. But the rapid intensity of their relationship had obviously proved too much.

Reluctant to grow up so quickly, Wilmer wanted to enjoy his youth. 'I didn't want to go out so much to premières and stuff, and he did,' Lindsay lamented. 'It was kind of like a tug of war.' The admission would come as quite a surprise to gossipmongers who already labelled Lindsay as an insatiable party animal. If her words were anything to go by, it seemed quite the opposite was true. 'The thing is, because I was younger, people made it out to be like I was the immature one,' said Lindsay afterwards. 'But, you know, it wasn't true. I wanted to stay home sometimes and he wanted to go out all the time.'

Both parties had very different objectives for the relationship; Lindsay was desperate to settle down and Wilmer wasn't. He'd chosen to exit altogether. According to Wilmer's friends, the break-up 'had to do with their work'. One source let it leak that Wilmer was frightened of the relationship souring, and damaging his career in the process, just like the acrimonious split between J-Lo and Ben Affleck. He later complained to the tabloids that his relationship with Lindsay had 'hurt his career'.

Although Lindsay tried to put on a brave face, she couldn't deny that the break-up had left her devastated. 'Wilmer was my first love, so it will take some time to get over him,' she said matter-of-factly. She even drew comparisons with her own family breakdown. 'Every break-up is painful, whether it's a boyfriend or your parents' marriage.'

Constant reminders in the press made it additionally difficult for Lindsay to deal with the heartache. 'He keeps talking about it in the papers,' she complained.

Dina sympathised with her daughter's anguish, but was convinced Lindsay would soon bounce back. 'When you're 18 and it's your first love, it hurts,' she mused. 'They are both so busy and they are so young. Wilmer was her first boyfriend, really, at an older age, so that's got to be tough on anyone. It's going to be sad. It's going to be, you know, relief... a lot of different emotions for both of them.'

Fellow teen star Ashlee Simpson agreed: 'It always sucks when you lose your first love.'

Lindsay already knew her friends, family and work would help her to regain some focus. 'That will help me get through it,' she proclaimed optimistically. Lindsay realised that her obsession with Wilmer had clouded her judgement. Desperate to spend every second of the day with her man, she'd drifted farther apart from her friends. 'Your whole life becomes about them, and you lose touch with your friends,' she admitted. Now would be an opportunity to rebuild those relationships if it wasn't already too late. Lindsay wanted to find herself again.

In a bid to retain their friendship, both parties attempted to stay silent on their reasons for the split. But, with time, snippets of information filtered through to the press. Lindsay later confessed that the relationship had become 'too much work'. 'Being in a relationship should never be work. If there's work, then you should get out of it.'

But Lindsay later hinted that a much more serious issue of trust lay at the root of their problems. In the past, Lindsay had complained to friends about the number of beautiful women who would approach Wilmer. 'It's hard when we go out,' she complained.

'They'll seriously hit on him right in front of me. I'm already insecure and there are a lot of pretty girls in LA. It makes me feel bad.'

Exhausted in both her work and personal life, Lindsay's insecurities would only grow. Ever since she arrived in Hollywood, she'd felt like the odd one out. Convinced Wilmer would leave her, she started to distrust him. 'There were all these girls around... he would flirt with them, and I couldn't handle that. I really didn't trust him.' Looking back, Lindsay admitted, 'My life was too out of order. I was too depressed. I was too concerned with Wilmer this, Wilmer that.'

Initially bitter about being dumped, Lindsay ran through a gamut of emotions. Eventually, she reconciled herself with the age-old adage that to have loved and lost is better than to have never loved at all. She had learned a lot in her relationship with Wilmer and none of that would be wasted. 'At my age, to have been able to feel the way I did about Wilmer... I'm so grateful to have had that. It taught me to be more comfortable with myself.'

As a pledge of her gratitude, Lindsay decided to keep a special love note in the liner notes to her début album *Speak*. The note read, 'Wilmer, thank you for being by my side whenever I need you.' Lindsay also included the following message for her father: 'Papi, thanks for telling me I can do it all and for being proud. Thank you for loving me. I love you.'

Obviously in a reflective mood, Lindsay was clearly taking an opportunity to air the skeletons in her closet. Like anyone experiencing their first break-up, Lindsay now understood a lot more about the mysterious world of relationships. 'Girls don't get how insecure guys can be,' she told one girly magazine. 'Guys just hold it in better, which makes them even more insecure. They have to play it like they don't care because that's the guy thing. But the more girls understand that, the more confident they will get in their relationship.'

Obviously on a roll, she continued, 'The thing is, girls ultimately control the relationship – and I have guys tell me that as well. Sure, the guy is going to think other girls are hot, but guys are always afraid of girls breaking up with them. So it's really a two-way street. A guy wants a girl who is confident and shows she's independent and doesn't always need him.' It didn't take a genius to work out that Lindsay was indulging in self-analysis. Tellingly, she revealed, 'I went through a phase where I became so dependent on other people and guys I liked that I was completely not myself.'

But Lindsay was not about to start beating herself up for having feelings. She was proud of the way she'd handled her first break-up. 'I think being sensitive is a good thing, because it shows we have feelings. I have no problem letting my feelings show, and sometimes it's bad. But, if I feel a certain way, then I'm going to tell that person. Because, if I hold my feelings in, it's going to be that much worse when I finally do say something.'

In all aspects of her life, Lindsay had reached a new level of maturity. Given time to mull over her emotions, she appeared quite sanguine about the whole affair. 'I'm kind of over it as much as I can be, but still hoping there's a way to work things out,' she said with unabashed honesty. 'We still really love each other, and maybe one day we'll be back together, maybe not. It's all up to fate.'

Being friends wasn't easy, but Lindsay was adult enough to give it her best shot. 'We're on different levels now; we're just really different people. Time has passed and you realise and see it and know. I'm just me. I have my work, my album, my filming. I'm making sure I'm OK with everyone.'

Subsequently, Lindsay and Wilmer remained friends. But reports suggested an attraction that still existed between the two. One evening, they both showed up at LA's Mood club. Despite choosing to sit in separate VIP rooms, talk of romance still prevailed. According to sources, the pair left through different exits and later met up outside.

A few weeks later, Lindsay also reneged on a promotional appointment to spend time with Wilmer, further stoking rumours of a reunion.

According to the organisers of new fashion line People's Liberation, the troubled star had assured them she would attend a launch party at plush LA club Nacional. But, at the last minute, Lindsay dropped out to dine with her former boyfriend at Mr Chow. When journalists confronted the star with the suggestion that their relationship might be back on, she simply rolled her eyes and replied, 'That's so over.' She went on to explain, 'It's all mumbo-jumbo, yadda yadda yadda. I'm not back with Wilmer. Listen, we're just friends. It was really hard for us to get to a place where we could actually be on a friendly level again, because there were so many people who had a perception of what our relationship was like. He's someone who had a big impact on my life. I had to get him back in my life. You should always be able to have a relationship with someone who was a love of yours.'

Meanwhile, rumours that Wilmer might be getting back with his ex-girlfriend Mandy Moore had started to do the rounds. Lindsay was left feeling confused. 'I don't know if she knows that Wilmer has been hanging out with Mandy,' an undisclosed source told the tabloids. 'That was always one of the trouble spots in their relationship. It was that threatening ex-girlfriend-type thing.'

But Mandy Moore's spokespeople were quick to refute any allegations. 'Mandy and Wilmer dated for a year, and they're still friends, but she's with someone else now, and they're hurt by the rumour,' said a spokeswoman.

Lindsay was also linked to several high-profile stars including Wilmer's friend Armani model Clarence Fuller. A gossip column reported how Lindsay had invited Clarence to join her at the New York club Marquee, before moving on to another club, Suede, and finally her hotel suite. 'Lindsay has had her eye on him for a while, but she was always in a relationship before,' said a so-called friend. But, when confronted about the story, Lindsay merely replied, 'Clarence who?' Hitting out at reports, she later made a joke of the suggestion by wearing a T-shirt with the phrase 'You were never my boyfriend' when the pair co-hosted MTV's *Total Request Live*.

Even more hurtfully, Lindsay was linked to Stavros Niarchos, ex-boyfriend of Mary-Kate Olsen, and Paris Hilton's current squeeze. 'That's 100 per cent not true,' blasted her representatives. 'Lindsay is very good friends with Mary-Kate, and she is appalled that Paris is dating Stavros.'

But Lindsay gave gossips even more ammunition when she was spotted eyeing up jewellery at Harry Winston in New York. Staff insisted, however, that she was merely shopping for herself. 'One of the first things Lindsay said was, "I love Jennifer Lopez... and

I love the pink diamond she got from Harry Winston, and I want a pink diamond just like it,"' assured a member of staff. After trying on a $1.5 million (£789,470) oval diamond, Lindsay left with a few donated gems intended for wear at several promotional engagements.

While Lindsay was clearly upset about the split, she was determined not to sit around and mope at home. The best way to deal with her heartache was to keep busy and that meant hitting the clubs in a big way! Whereas Lindsay had been content to stay indoors with Wilmer, she was now determined to spend more time with her friends.

Along with high-profile pals like Paris Hilton, the Olsens and socialite Bijou Phillips, she was sighted at a string of celebrity LA clubs. She was unwittingly stepping into the 'It' girl mould so carefully crafted for her by the media. Eagerly, tabloids soaked up the stories of late-night endeavours and extravagant escapades. Whispers suggested Lindsay was on a mission to find herself a new high-profile boyfriend to punish Wilmer. Lindsay argued she was simply 'having fun' and wasn't interested in finding another boyfriend. 'I'm not going from dating someone I was in love with just to be dating someone else. I'm not dating anyone,' she said defiantly. 'I'm afraid to hang out with any guys now because [the tabloids] say I'm dating people that I hang out with.'

Days after she'd been discharged from hospital, Lindsay had bounced back on the party circuit. Tales of liaisons with older men and underage drinking were reported in the press. 'Black guys love me,' she boasted. 'Damon Dash, P Diddy, 50 [Cent] called my agent for my number. He said he was watching *Mean Girls* and loved it. I was freaking out!'

Lindsay was a big fan of hip-hop and counted Eminem and 50 Cent among her idols. Earlier in the year, when Lindsay was presenting the MTV Movie Awards, she had been desperate to hook up with Eminem. 'I thought we might meet, but we didn't get the chance,' she complained. 'A couple of people told me he wanted to meet me but I was so busy. I saw him just before I went on stage and we kind of smiled at each other. Once the show was over and everything settled down, I couldn't quite believe that he had wanted to meet me. I'd love to do a song with him.'

Intrigued, but perhaps a little frightened, Lindsay followed up on 50's phone call. The hard-knocks gangster rapper suggested that Lindsay came down to his video shoot on Long Island. Having seen Eminem verbally attack teen stars such as Britney and Christina Aguilera in his videos, Lindsay wasn't quite sure what to expect. 'I was scared he was going to make fun and be really mean, but he wasn't – he was really nice.' 50 even invited Lindsay to appear in the video, but she declined. 'My brother was so mad at me!' she laughed.

Nothing ever evolved romantically, but the pair did strike up a friendship and Lindsay even affectionately refers to the rapper as her 'home dog'.

Surprisingly, Lindsay was better known in the rap community than she was among her own Hollywood peers. Lindsay confesses one of her most embarrassing celebrity-related moments to be the time she ran over to Brad Pitt 'like a stalker' during the première of *Mr and Mrs Smith*. Brad was signing autographs for fans when Lindsay spotted him on the red carpet. Lindsay had always been a fan herself and couldn't let this golden opportunity escape her. At the very least, she had to say hello to Brad Pitt – if only to make all her friends in New York jealous. For a split-second, Lindsay Lohan was no longer a demure celebrity; she was a dumbstruck teenager who couldn't believe her luck. She ran straight over and tapped Brad on the shoulder. Somewhat embarrassingly, he didn't have a clue who Lindsay was. 'I said, "I just have to introduce myself... " He didn't know who I was, and [then] he was like, "Ohhh..."'

Fortunately, Lindsay could see the funny side. Anyway, she would later reveal that it wasn't Brad Pitt she had a crush on – but his girlfriend Angelina Jolie! 'He's beautiful, but I've got more of a crush on Angelina than Brad!' she laughed. 'She's sexy as hell!'

In fact, Lindsay repeated her stalker trick when she spied Angelina at the same première. 'I'm infatuated with Angelina... I ran up to her on the red carpet. The more advice I can get from these successful women the better.'

Lindsay also admired Angelina's work for humanitarian causes. Charitable work was something Lindsay believed all celebrities or people in a position of power should be involved with. 'I think she's one of those rare people who gives back as much as she does, not because of the press or because of any kind of attention she gets, but because it makes her feel better.'

It wasn't the first time Lindsay had chased after one of her heroes. As a child, she recalls going to the première of *Anywhere But Here* with her mum. 'While we were driving on the street, we saw Julia Roberts!' she exclaimed. 'I told my mom to stop the car but I got too embarrassed so we drove away! Julia Roberts is one of my favourite actresses, so I'm regretting it to this day.'

Now Lindsay was on a roll. She loved being a key mover on the club scene. She had so many new friends to hang out with, there simply weren't enough days in the week to fulfil all her invites. One night, the young star partied so hard she even misplaced her bag containing her Californian driver's licence and black American Express card. It was eventually tracked down at a college party in a Manhattan bar. On another occasion, a newspaper reported that Lindsay had footed the bill for a round of lemon drop shots and two bottles of vodka while partying with ten friends at New York nightspot Serena.

By now, everyone had a Lindsay Lohan story to tell. Even old associates were crawling out of the woodwork, eager to dish some dirt. Actress Megan Fox, Lindsay's co-star on *Confessions of a Teenage Drama Queen*, told *FHM* magazine that Lindsay would often ask her to buy cigarettes. 'Lindsay and I weren't the best of friends,' she said. 'Because I looked older than her, she'd be nice to my face. I would buy her cigarettes. We got away with it every time.'

Lindsay lashed out. 'I'm learning, and I'd rather make my own mistakes and learn from them than have to be sheltered my whole life,' she fumed.

Fortunately, not everyone wanted to take a shot at Lindsay. Plenty of her close pals were more than ready to defend the pressurised star. Glamorous heiress Paris Hilton protested, 'She's just adorable. She's 18 years old. If you're invited to these parties and can go, why not go? Who cares? She's young and she works her butt off doing all these movies. All we do is go out and dance and that's it. We love it!'

Her friend Jamie Gleicher, star of reality-TV show *Rich Girls*, agreed. 'To call her a saint wouldn't be fair to her. She knows she's not a saint, but she's not as wild as people think. If there's anything Lindsay does in excess it's dance. She loves to dance.'

In fact, Lindsay herself would be the first to admit that she loved the dance floor. 'I go to a club and, yeah, sometimes dance on a stool just because it's fun. I'm not a bad girl – I just like to have fun. I don't think I've ever been perceived as one of those perfect girls. I'm only human.'

Still below the legal age for alcohol consumption, Lindsay's tipple of choice was usually nothing stronger than a Red Bull. She did confess to indulging in the odd drink or two, but nothing on the scale of newspaper reports. 'If I go out in New York or something with my friends, I'll have a drink, I'm not going to lie,' she sighed. 'But it's not like I order bottles of vodka to my table or order drinks. Most of my friends are over 21, and if I have a sip or whatever it's not a big deal. It's not like I order things to my table and get wasted and all trashed.'

Besides, Lindsay cared too much for her image to make a fool of herself in public. 'Having a drink is one thing, because the more people try to shield you from that, the more you're going to want to rebel and do it. [But] I've never wanted to exceed my limit. It's not fun to go to a party and lose control of yourself and get sick. It makes you look stupid. You want to be the mature one who's not going to do that – especially if you like a guy. It's always better not to be the person at the party who's wasted. That's embarrassing.'

Growing up in the public eye was difficult. Often, Lindsay thought it unfair that, while most of her friends were out having a good time, she was being punished for even stepping through a club doorway. 'My friends are in college now and they're going to frat parties and drinking beer,' she complained. 'But [they're] out getting wasted and I don't really have a desire to do that. I have sort of grown past it because I have a full-time job and responsibilities. It's cool to have that; it makes you mature faster.'

Lindsay also felt victimised. Why was everyone suddenly picking on her? 'Ashlee Simpson, Hilary Duff... they've been going to the same clubs I'm at, but you never hear about it. But, when I do it, it's front-page news! I'm an angel compared to many of my friends!'

Supporting her daughter's integrity, Dina agreed that the press had blown everything out of proportion. 'If anything, Lindsay is a late bloomer. To go to a club when you're 18 is not ridiculous.' As far as she was concerned, there was nothing to worry about; she trusted Lindsay implicitly and often the pair would go out partying together.

'My mom is the coolest person ever!' boasted Lindsay. 'I like going to dinner with her and having my friends over with her. My mom's just the best and I love her to death.'

Whenever a fresh story of scandalous behaviour hit the headlines, a distraught Lindsay would turn to her mother. 'If there's something printed that's wrong, she calls and says, "Mommy, I can't believe they wrote this,"' recounted Dina. 'I say, "You're at the top. There's a price for everything. You can't cry and whine. You're a star."'

According to Dina, it was simply Lindsay's honesty that got her into trouble. 'She's honest to a fault. She's naive in a lot of ways.'

But Lindsay refused to compromise her lifestyle and crumble under pressure from the press. 'I'm the type of person who doesn't really hide anything,' she fumed. 'I go to clubs and everything and, if I hang out with Paris Hilton, I don't think that's a bad thing. She's a nice girl. I relieve my stress by going out and having fun.'

Fired up, she continued, 'Some people may go and take a yoga class, but people don't care about that. I'll be in LA and, if I drive to the gym, they take that picture but they never use it because that doesn't sell… because people like the drama. That's kind of what Hollywood's become in a way, as sad as it is, especially for younger girls. We have 18-year-olds that go to war, and they can't even have a drink. So what does that say about society? I mean, what does it really say? So then when you have an 18-year-old in Hollywood, at a party, and maybe she sees drugs on a table...'

Unfortunately, 'honesty' didn't shift newspaper units, so, in the eyes of the press, Lindsay remained a Hollywood wild child. But, as stories of underage drinking began to lose their impact, tales of substance abuse took their place. Drugs were quickly linked to Lindsay's mystery hospitalisation and her subsequent weight loss. She denied the rumours emphatically. 'Now that I'm getting older, people are trying to say I'm into drugs, that I party all the time – just, like, silly stuff,' she complained. 'I don't do drugs – never have, never will. I don't need to do that stuff to have fun.'

Lindsay was beginning to resent the new party-girl tag she'd been given. 'I hate the term "party girl",' she seethed. 'I'd use it for someone I have no respect for. It offends me.'

Since living in Hollywood, she'd witnessed her fair share of scandalous activity but didn't want to be lumped into a category of reckless socialites. Without mentioning names, she drew reference to other young Hollywood stars. 'Some of them make rumours up about other girls in the business,' she whispered conspiratorially. 'They'll say, "Oh, she does drugs... she drinks too much... " I know a lot of the girls in LA smoke pot, but I can't do that. I would have an asthma attack.'

Lindsay even slammed reports she was a smoker. 'It's stupid to smoke… I do that once in a while, but everyone goes through that phase.'

Like any young girl, Lindsay was concerned people might have the wrong impression about her. 'I'm sensitive and I have feelings,' she said. 'But I really believe I'm not doing anything to bother anyone else. I'm just doing my own thing.' As she quite rightly pointed out, she wasn't really doing anything wrong. 'It's not as if I'm married and I'm cheating on my husband. It's not like I'm robbing people or being a bitch. I get really hurt when I read those stories. Because I have to admit that I want people to like me. I want them to know that I'm not that horrible, selfish, out-of-control person that they keep reading about. I work hard, then I chill with my friends. I lead a fairly normal life.'

Her main concern was that prospective directors might doubt her commitment to an acting career. 'It hurts me because I don't want people having the wrong idea of what kind of person I am, that I'm immature and I'm not focused. I feel like I'm very sincere, and I don't take anything for granted. I feel blessed and lucky, and I'm appreciative and I'm thankful, and I'm not some crazy, Tara Reid-esque party girl. I want to be in this for the long run.'

In the past, Lindsay had been careful not to mention names in her assault on Hollywood, but her

Lindsay at the premiere of *Herbie: Fully Loaded*. Lindsay's health suffered dramatically on the shoot, and rumours abounded about her subsequent weight loss.

Young love…

Above left: Lindsay's first high profile boyfriend, singer and actor Aaron Carter – she later described the relationship as 'puppy love'.

Above right: Wilmer again in happier times – after her mother Dina, Lindsay had always turned to Wilmer for support, and the break-up hit her hard.

Below: New love or just a rumour? Lindsay has been romantically linked with actor Jared Leto.

Hitting the town…
Enjoying the nightlife in New York and LA, with her friend Paris Hilton (below right).
Lindsay has developed something of a reputation as a party girl, a tag she is reluctant to
accept, saying simply that she's young and having fun.

Multi-talented – Lindsay realised her dream of crossing over and becoming a pop star as well as a movie star.

Above: At Manhattan's Hit Factory where her first TV singing appearance was recorded.

Below: At the 2005 American Music Awards in LA.

Above: After a shaky start to her pop career, Lindsay became a confident live performer.

Below: Performing at Times Square, New York on New Year's Eve 2005.

Above: Looking good – Lindsay dazzles the catwalk modelling for Calvin Klein.

Below: 'It's great to be single!' Lindsay declares her love for the single lifestyle, aping Tom Cruise in the process, on the *Tonight Show*.

And the winner is… Lindsay goes wild after winning Best Female Actress for *Mean Girls* at the 2005 MTV Movie Awards.

A family affair…

Above: Lindsay's father Michael in court again, this time seeking a cut of his daughter's earnings in response to Dina's divorce suit.

Below left: Dina with Aliana and Dakota – both growing up fast!

Below right: Lindsay and her mother, looking towards a bright future – 'My mom's just the best and I love her to death!'

comments about Tara Reid evoked outrage from the *American Pie* star. It was true, Tara was famed for her hedonistic lifestyle and seemed to have taken up permanent residency in showbiz columns; only weeks earlier, she'd made headline news when her breast fell out of her dress on the red carpet of P Diddy's 35th birthday party. But she resented any association with Lindsay Lohan. 'A tabloid reported she moved into my house and she's never even been to my house!' fumed Tara. 'Some article said I was a bad influence on her, because she was going out and going crazy. But Lindsay Lohan is way more wild than I was when I was her age. Don't put me with her – I don't want to be dragged into her shit.'

Lindsay experienced the full force of Tara's anger when she attempted to introduce herself at a dinner party with Paris Hilton. Needless to say, she was greeted with a frosty reception. Lindsay recalls, 'She showed up at dinner in Las Vegas, and Paris said hi to me and didn't say hi to Tara, so she freaked out and was like, "I'm going to fucking kill you!" And I was like, "Hi, I'm Lindsay, nice to meet you."'

At a later date, however, both girls would dismiss the apparent discord as pure speculation. 'Oh, there's nothing there. It's like, if it's not Hilary, it's Tara,' said Lindsay.

Tara agreed, 'It's crazy. It's so not true. Everyone keeps talking about it.'

Already, Lindsay's life in Hollywood was starting to resemble the script from her blockbuster movie *Mean Girls*. 'Everyone is friends,' she said of the complicated and incestuous network. 'It's like a big high school – that's what Los Angeles is, and now New York, too, and Miami and even New Orleans. Everyone that's out, you know them from being at parties and being on red carpets and being at events, and everyone is friends.'

More than anything, Lindsay needed a dose of normal life. The Thanksgiving holiday celebrations granted the ideal opportunity for rest and relaxation. Lindsay chartered a private jet for her friends and assistants to fly in for the holidays. 'The fact that I could do that was the coolest thing in the world!' she said of the grand gesture. But multimillion-dollar movie star or not, Lindsay wouldn't be getting any star treatment at home. 'She's coming home for Thanksgiving,' confirmed Dina. 'She better help me cook. I'm having everyone. She's got to help. When she's home, she's Lindsay. She's Lindsay the big sister, you know, yelling at Ali… we're just normal.'

At least for five days, Lindsay could enjoy life as a normal teenager. She needed to make the most of it, because very soon she'd be back to work.

13

SPEAK FROM THE HEART

Almost overshadowed by all the drama of the past few months, Lindsay's professional career had been ticking along nicely. All the hard work she had almost killed herself doing was now finally coming to fruition. While already established as an actress, Lindsay was preparing to release her début album *Speak*. Although her working environment hadn't been ideal, she was happy with the result. 'I wanted the album to come off like a burned CD made by a girl. I wanted it to be something you could listen to when you're out with your friends or dance to or be depressed to,' she explained. 'I just wanted to talk about myself and what I go through, that's why I called it *Speak* – speak about love, hate, everything that goes on in your life,' she said of the lyrical content. 'My music is not a character, it's not someone I've written about – it's just me, Lindsay.'

Lindsay hoped people would respect her sincerity and give her the opportunity to shine. 'People don't have to rave about it, but I want it to touch people whatever way it will touch the people individually.'

Although she was an international movie star, Lindsay was nervous about making the transition to becoming a pop star. There was also a risk that people would take her less seriously as an actress. 'I guess everyone's going to have their own opinion, and I'm doing it because it's something that I want to do,' said Lindsay. 'And, while I'm young, I feel like it's the time to do it and have fun and experiment.'

That said, Lindsay would argue that her acting career was still in the early stages. 'I don't think I've proved myself as an actor yet – yeah, maybe in the box office for kids in the States. But I need to find pieces that really show I can act.'

Musically, Lindsay wanted the record to reflect her own diverse tastes. Speaking about her interests, she said, 'I have The Beatles! And John Lennon – I do! And I have Journey and The Smiths. I also have Keane and Fru Fru, and The Garden State soundtrack is my favourite and The Dave Matthews Band new CD. But then I also have 50 Cent and Eminem. A good balance. I have everything. I have all types of music. I like country. I like everything.'

The final product Lindsay came up with was a slick collection of pop-rock tunes, perfect for MTV. Choosing the content and direction for her album had been tricky. Although Lindsay was growing up quickly in the press, much of her fan base was still young. Creatively, she'd reached a point where she wanted to discuss more adult issues, but it was also important not to alienate her younger fans. 'It's hard because I want to sing specific lyrics and dress a certain way and act a certain way in videos but still make sure that all of those things are appropriate to my fans.' Often, she used her younger sister Ali as a gauge of suitable material.

Ultimately, most of the songs on *Speak* gave a biographical account of being Lindsay Lohan. It's no real surprise that she chose to dedicate her début single 'Rumors' to the paparazzi who had hounded her so intensively for the past few months. 'I'm tired of rumours starting… I'm sick of being followed… I'm tired of people lying, saying what they want about me… I gotta say respectfully, I would love it if you would take the camera off of me…' she sings.

On the set of her début video shoot, Lindsay explained the premise of the song. 'A lot of people have put out rumours about me being a party girl and stuff. People were writing things. It was starting to hurt me – saying I had fake breasts, all this stupid shit. It got to a point where it was like, OK, I'm 17 years old, I don't have implants. And they were saying I was 23. So the song made sense. [The song's] basically just saying I do go out with my friends and this is exactly what happens when I go out at night. I go and I dance and I have fun and then I leave.'

Admittedly, Lindsay had been the victim of several unsubstantiated rumours. Alongside the party-girl allegations, there was also a suggestion the young singer might be lying about her age. One newspaper reported that Lindsay was, in fact, 23 years old. 'All my friends heard it on Long Island and they called me,' she said. 'It's flattering that people want to know so much about me and want to take the time to make up that many things about me.'

The most ridiculous rumour to date, however, involved an incident in a bakery and a blueberry muffin! Lindsay explained the bizarre story. 'Oh my God, there was this ridiculous rumour that I went to a bakery shop in Santa Monica and that I wanted a blueberry muffin and there were none left, so I had a fit in the bakery and asked some girl if I could have hers or just took it from her, or something like that,' she blurted, almost with laughter. 'First of all, I don't really eat muffins. And, second, I'm allergic to blueberries!'

While Lindsay had developed a thick skin for dealing with stories, she was angry about the way they affected her family. Attempts to shield her younger sister from the salacious gossip were futile. Too young to properly understand, she'd often wonder if such stories were really true. 'My little sister's always wanted to do everything I do, and now she reads the tabloid magazines, so anything she sees she usually calls me, either crying or yelling at me,' said Lindsay, a note of anger in her voice. 'She's like, "My friends saw this… they read this… and they saw that you were doing this…" or "You were at a club…" and "Are you even allowed to do that?"'

Subsequently, Lindsay was extremely self-conscious about her conduct in the outside world. At the same time, however, she wanted to project the image of a normal teenager. 'You have to find who you are and not really care what other people think. That's the best thing that you can do. I want to be normal; I want to be like any person my age.'

While critics were curious as to what material Lindsay would turn up, socialites had already pencilled in a date for her début album launch party. The event would take place at New York's Marquee club. All afternoon, Lindsay had been deliberating over a choice of outfit, before finally settling for a slinky cocktail dress. She arrived at the club to find images of herself plastered all over the walls. Thanks to computer technology, there was not a freckle in sight. 'It doesn't look like me 'cause I'm all tanned and stuff,' she giggled. 'I have no freckles at all in that shot. The magic of technology!'

Aside from a few close friends, the celebrity count was surprisingly low. Contrary to press rumour, Lindsay remained completely sober. In fact, the affair was fairly understated. The only shocked gasps of the evening came when P Diddy made a surprise entrance. Lindsay had befriended the music mogul on New York's social scene and insisted he drop in. 'I was like, "You have to come by,"' said Lindsay later. 'He was like, "Oh, I don't know… I don't feel well," but he showed up. He's really sweet. He's actually very shy.'

Lindsay's priorities were called into question once again, however, when she cancelled a string of interviews to promote *Speak*. Only the night before, she'd been spotted out partying with Justin Timberlake. Her publicist blamed laryngitis, while Dina stressed that Lindsay had made every effort to meet her obligations. 'We have been working day and night.'

After a brief rest period, Lindsay made up for lost time and immersed herself fully in promo for the album. Her first TV singing appearance was a taping for *Sessions@AOL* recorded at Manhattan's Hit Factory. Excited about performing, she arrived in good humour. When the band started playing the wrong track to her second single 'Over', the guitarist joked, 'It's the drummer's fault!' making an amusing reference to Ashlee Simpson's recent lip-synch scandal on *Saturday Night Live*. Playing along with the joke, Lindsay did a stupid dance and the room erupted with laughter.

Just days later, however, Lindsay was herself accused of miming after performing two tracks from her album on popular TV show *Good Morning America*. Already lacking confidence in her musical ability, it came as a great blow to Lindsay. Thousands of viewers phoned in to complain that the singer had mimed her words and missed her cues. But her representatives claimed that Lindsay had simply been using a backing track for guide vocals. 'All musical artists that perform on *Good Morning America* are required to perform live,' added a spokeswoman for the show. 'On occasion, artists will have a backing track to support their live vocals.'

Ever the optimist, Dina remained upbeat about the performance. 'It was her first time performing live, so it was really cool.'

Lindsay addressed the issue in a later interview. She insisted that choosing songs she was capable of singing live had been integral to the process of selecting tracks for her album. 'My main concern was to sing songs that, when I sing live, it sounds the same and I don't have to worry about it and I don't have to stress my voice. I wanna be able to sing stuff to show that I have a voice and I can actually project.'

Although embarrassed, Lindsay handled the situation with remarkable professionalism. In the grand scheme of things, questionable live performances were actually the last thing on her mind – she had far greater problems at home to contend with. Once again, her father was in hot water with the police, causing her family distress and heartache. On this occasion, he'd broken the protection order a judge had enforced back in October. Desperate to see his daughter, Michael had turned up at her younger brother's soccer game in Merrick, Long Island. He saw Lindsay through the window of a black BMW, which immediately pulled away, and he instructed his own driver to follow it. But, when he caught up with the car at traffic lights, he was shocked to discover Dina in the back seat. Technically, Michael was not allowed anywhere near his estranged wife.

Subsequently, he was charged and released without bail. Refusing to take heed, two weeks later he violated the order again when he pulled into Dina's driveway in Merrick. Dina's security guards called the police and he was held in custody after police determined he was drunk.

Fed up with Michael's flagrant disregard for the law, the judge set bail at a whopping $1 million – the same amount usually placed on a murder suspect. Additionally, Michael was charged with driving under the influence and forced to remain in jail until he could stump up $500,000 of the bail money in cash. At the family's request, Dina's protection order was also extended to include Lindsay and her siblings.

Financially and emotionally, it was a severe blow for Michael. During a hearing, he collapsed from chest pains and a shortness of breath, causing the case to be adjourned. It was the second time he'd suffered health problems in the courtroom, having previously experienced the same occurrence back in June. Officers rushed Michael to Winthrop-University Hospital for tests on his heart. But he wasn't about to escape lightly; they ensured he was firmly handcuffed to his bed.

Michael believed he had been set up. He became concerned that forces were conspiring to keep him from his family and pointed the finger directly at his brother-in-law. Speaking about his violation of the protection orders, he claimed to have made arrangements with a police escort to collect some of his clothes. He was simply waiting for the car to arrive at the time he was busted. Michael was even convinced members of Dina's family were actually travelling in the police patrol car that picked him up.

Fortunately for Michael, his lawyer intervened in the courtroom. She argued that he had simply visited the house to see his son and pick up some clothes. At the time, Cody was not included in the protection order a judge had set. 'He called the police to tell them he was going there. And he was going to see his son, where there was no order of protection,' it was claimed in evidence. Michael's lawyer also made a point of stating that her client had tested negative for 'every single drug possible'. In light of those facts, she vowed to appeal against the bail amount. 'In my 35 years of practising law... this is the highest bail I've ever seen in a domestic case. If it wasn't for him having a rich movie-star daughter, it would never have been like that,' she complained.

But the court disagreed. Michael Lohan had repeatedly broken the law and it was too late to show any remorse. He was found guilty and sentenced to 28 days at Conifer Park, a treatment facility for alcohol and substance abuse. As he packed his things and prepared to leave, he joked he was in a strait-jacket.

Lindsay and her family were relieved. Although they were worried for Michael, at least now they could enjoy some peace over the Christmas period. Ironically, it would be Lindsay's busiest time ever. Now a fully fledged singer and film star, she was in high demand over the festive season. On New Year's Eve, she even agreed to attend two different engagements at opposite ends of the country. Any resolutions to reduce her workload were quickly disappearing. First, she would perform on MTV's *Total Request Live* in New York and then she would fly by private jet to Miami, Florida, where she would

SPEAK FROM THE HEART

host a party at South Beach's Opium Garden with Jessica Alba. Given the traffic to and from both airports, sceptics wondered if she'd turn up at all! Of course, she cruised it.

As for Christmas gifts, Lindsay had one very special request – that the press leave her alone. 'If I could have one thing for the holidays, it would be for no tabloids to write anything about me,' she begged. It was a nice thought but, unfortunately, even the richest girls can't have everything they want. Very soon, Lindsay would be back in the limelight and she needed to be prepared – 2005 was going to be her toughest year yet.

14

BREAKING THE MOULD

One of Lindsay's key ambitions for 2005 was to make the transition to an older audience. Although she now had a strong teen following, the Disney roles she'd previously been offered didn't really allow the ambitious star to flex her acting muscles fully. For a long time, she'd felt overshadowed by stars like Natalie Portman and Kirsten Dunst, who were taken more seriously in the film industry. It was a question of earning potential; Lindsay's agents had already brokered $7.5 million for her next film role and were looking at $10 or even $15 million thereafter. What Lindsay really yearned for was critical respect. 'The stuff that I've been doing, I haven't really been able to act yet,' she complained, ignoring all the fantastic reviews she constantly received for her comedic performances. 'I want to really act in a film and commit to something and be a different person. The characters I've played so far are very similar to who I am, so it's hard to say that I'm actually fully acting. I want to find something that's a little bit more dramatic, something that's different from what I usually do.'

To some extent, Lindsay knew she'd already been typecast as the thoughtful redhead who triumphs over adversity and learns from her experience. The financial success of her last few films made her a sure-fire hit in the pre-teen market. But Lindsay was keen to break the mould and explore new territories. 'I don't want to give an image of doing only teen movies and just being this perfect teen. Other girls my age – like Evan Rachel Wood and Scarlett Johansson and even Mischa Barton – they've done riskier roles. And, fashion-wise, they become these icons. I could do that, but people won't take me as seriously. It's hard to get around that.'

Lindsay's agents were already pushing her to screen test for riskier roles. But, on the advice of Dina, Lindsay was cautious about moving too quickly and therefore risking alienating her younger fans. She was presented with a script called *Margaret*, about a high-school student who has an affair with her African-American teacher and ends up having an abortion. Lindsay was really keen to accept the role but Dina insisted that, unless the writers agreed to cut some of the more controversial material, she wouldn't be taking it any further. 'It's really, really hard because I want to do this movie to show people that I can do that, because I know I can. But at the same time I don't know if I want to jump that far ahead. Do I want to risk having my little sister wanting to see a movie that I'm in, and me not wanting her to see it? And people being disappointed in me? I don't know. I'm in a hard place right now.'

Lindsay's sister Ali had become an important benchmark of what was deemed 'acceptable' in her career. As a role model, she felt a great sense of responsibility. 'A lot of what I do, I do for my sister. Because, once I grow up, I can't go back to these teen roles, these high-school roles where the characters are learning to be themselves.'

She was even sent a treatment for a film about *Deep Throat* porn star Linda Lovelace, but that was rejected instantly.

Lindsay knew she was in a tricky situation; suddenly leaping into a more dramatic role better suited to an actress her own age would probably confuse a lot of people. 'It's so weird, because I'm almost 18 and I'm afraid to play something drastically different,' she said, taking a very philosophical view. While Lindsay was aware younger actresses such as Dakota Fanning (who co-starred with Denzel Washington in *Man on Fire*) could get away with a lot more in their films, she remained limited by her audience. 'It's just the way you develop your career and the image you put out,' she concluded.

Although Dina recognised her daughter's ambition, she advised her to exercise caution. 'We can't push it too over the edge,' she said firmly.

But at the same time, Lindsay knew it would soon be time to make a break. After all, her exploits in the press were making her less of a favourable prospect to Disney. 'I've accumulated a lot of younger fans over the years and I don't want to send out the wrong message to them, but at the same time I also have to do what's right for me.'

Navigating her career towards a more adult audience would inevitably lead Lindsay into scenes of a more explicit sexual nature. But Lindsay still had plenty of reservations about filming sex scenes. 'I'm afraid to have a sex scene,' she admitted. 'I don't want to lose my virginity in a movie yet because then I can't go back. I want to grow with my films, not ahead of them. The second I lose them is the second people aren't going to see my movies.'

She was also reluctant to do any nude scenes, feeling they were often just a cheap sell. 'I don't think nude scenes are necessary for me. A lot of actresses do it and they're comfortable with it. But I feel like, what's it gonna change in the movie? Guys might want you more... ha ha. But that's not even acting, that's shooting porno.'

Needless to say, when *Playboy* approached the young star with the offer of a shoot she refused point-blank. 'I'm not doing *Playboy*, no… never. They contacted my publicist and they asked if I would do their 20 questions spread, which is not a nude photo that they do with it. It's a regular photo,' she explained.

In many ways, Lindsay was quite old-fashioned with her views. She idealised the glamour of '50s Hollywood, an era in the film industry that had spawned many of her acting heroes. 'I think everyone in general is overexposed,' she boldly claimed. 'Personally, I think it would be nice if the studios went back to how they used to be when they protected their actresses and girls actually wore more clothing. That may sound hypocritical because I like to wear sexy things sometimes, but that's just because the only things that people consider sexy right now is what's out there. If sexy was brought back in the way that Marilyn Monroe or Brigitte Bardot used to do it, then it might be different.'

In a more modern context, Lindsay hoped to follow in the footsteps of Julia Roberts, upon whom she was beginning to model her own career. 'I want to follow the career of Julia Roberts, who never had a sex scene in a movie to get an Oscar, who does all those romantic comedies. That's why people love her. That's the kind of acting I want to do.'

She went on to criticise actors who landed Oscars

with controversial film roles. 'With movies now, it's very easy for a girl to dumb herself down or look ugly or be naked or be a lesbian or gain weight – those are the ones that win Oscars. The only one who didn't have to do that was Julia Roberts. And she never took her clothes off.' Her somewhat naive comments were met with raised eyebrows.

What Lindsay really needed was a transitional role. As she put it herself, 'something that no one would expect from me'. That very role presented itself with the romantic comedy *Just My Luck*. Lindsay would play Ashley Albright, the luckiest girl in New York, who loses her lucky powers after falling in love with the unluckiest man in the world.

The director, Donald Petrie, had put Kate Hudson and Sandra Bullock through their paces in *How To Lose a Guy in 10 Days* and *Miss Congeniality*. Lindsay knew she was in good hands. Her character in the film was 23, the age tabloids had often alleged her to be, and Lindsay chose to play her 'very Lucille Ball-esque'. 'She's younger, she's getting promotions where she works and everything just goes really well for her all the time. She doesn't realise how lucky she is and kind of loses appreciation for the fact that she's lucky. Then she loses all of her luck after kissing someone. She goes to this tarot card reader at this party she's having and, basically, she has to go around Manhattan with pictures of all the guys she hired as dancers and find the guy that she kissed, to kiss him again and get her luck back.'

The film was definitely a change from the norm. '[It's] a great piece for me in terms of coming of age.' Admittedly, the young star was nervous about shooting her scenes. Some of them involved Lindsay rolling around in mud and simulating being executed. 'I got to go a little crazy, have my freak-out scenes,' she laughed. 'It's hard to do that [kind of stuff], with everyone on the set [watching]. You feel silly, but it's fun because you can let go and just free yourself. It's like therapy.'

Lindsay also enjoyed selecting outfits for her character. In contrast to the teeny-bopper outfits she was usually required to wear, her wardrobe reflected the new type of sophisticated character she was playing. 'It was nice to play a character who knows who Jimmy Choo is!' she quipped.

But filming so many love scenes came as a shock to the system. 'I don't think I realised how much kissing there would be when I first read the script,' admitted Lindsay. In one sequence, Lindsay's character attempts to recover her lucky powers by kissing every handsome man in New York. While plenty of girls would jump at the chance to lock lips with an army of good-looking actors, Lindsay felt uncomfortable. 'I felt very dirty doing that… kinda trampy,' she said afterwards. 'I said to Donald, "Can we fake it and shoot it from a different angle?" But Donald insisted Lindsay do the scenes properly. 'So I kissed a lot of guys, which was sometimes gross and sometimes funny. It wasn't a kiss-kiss, though… more of a smooch,' recalls Lohan. 'They weren't too shabby-looking. I got off easy.'

Lindsay agreed it was nice to do something different in her career, but the gender imbalance on set did throw her. 'I wasn't used to needing to have that much chemistry with someone day in and day out.'

According to rumours, there was plenty of chemistry taking place off screen as well. Lindsay was linked to 19-year-old British drummer Harry Judd, whose band McFly had been offered a cameo role in the film. The pair were apparently spotted in a romantic clinch at a party in Louisiana. An unnamed source reported, 'Harry had the hots for her the moment he saw her. They started off as friends, mucking around together on set and it has gone on from there.' But, once again, there appeared to be no substance to the story. Other members of the band laughed off reports. 'He wishes something was going on!' joked guitarist Danny Jones. 'I think he dreamed about it and then he was like, "Did I dream it or did it actually happen?"'

But that was just the beginning. Rumours about the newly single starlet were changing on a daily basis. The press claimed she had been conducting a secret affair with Christian Slater and that the *True Romance* star had been frequently spotted creeping into her trailer. Lindsay was disgusted by the insensitivity of journalists. Christian had only recently filed for divorce from his wife Ryan Haddon. Having experienced the effects of adultery in her own home life, she was hurt people might think her capable of such a thing. 'I know my dad's cheated on my mom and I could never be that person,' she fumed.

Even more bizarrely, Lindsay was linked to the producer of *Just My Luck*, actor Bruce Willis. Lindsay had allegedly been seen flirting with the 51-year-old at the launch party for his new film *Hostage*. Bruce Willis was equally shocked to hear reports he'd pulled down Lindsay's trousers to see her tattoo. While Lindsay had always stated a preference for older men, this was going a little too far. Bruce Willis was even older than her father! Both parties were horrified and embarrassed by the story. After all, they both had a professional relationship to maintain. 'She is not interested in Bruce Willis in any way but as the producer of her next film,' Lindsay's publicist firmly told the press.

Potentially more damaging rumours began to circulate about Lindsay's behaviour on set. There were whispers that her extravagant party lifestyle was starting to interfere with her work and that she often arrived at the studio looking tired and irritable. Several movie extras were even quoted anonymously in the *New Orleans Times-Picayune*, complaining of how she had allegedly turned the movie set into a daily hell. When Lindsay heard news of the reports, she was visibly stricken. 'Where is this being said?' she demanded, trembling with anger. 'Are you serious? Well, if I were a nightmare, I don't think I'd be doing it. I think it would be a karma issue. But that sucks and I don't want to know about it.'

Exhausted by the constant need to justify herself, she continued, 'You know, I have so much shit on my plate that, if I'm having a bad day and you aren't sympathetic towards that and I'm sympathetic towards you when you have your bad days, then I may say something to you, and I won't regret it. But people have been great on this movie. People really have, and it's been cool.'

Several magazines also reproduced unfounded rumours about her alleged behaviour at photo shoots. Dina later explained that it was her intervention that was often misconstrued. Describing herself as a 'no' mum, she emphasised her responsibility to protect and safeguard her daughter's interests. Often, it was just impossible to please everyone.

Rapidly losing her patience with the press, Lindsay was finding it difficult to remain calm, although for the most part she tried to keep smiling. Only adding to her woes, the drivers involved in her fender bender last June were now planning to sue for 'pain, discomfort and physical disability'. All of this Lindsay could just about handle. But, when unfounded rumours started to surface that her ex-boyfriend Wilmer had become romantically involved with her supposed friend Ashlee Simpson, Lindsay was shocked.

When the break-up first happened, Lindsay turned to Ashlee for help. The singer offered to act as a mediator between Lindsay and Wilmer, helping the couple patch up their differences. But, according to US gossip rag *Star*, Ashlee had been busy hooking up with Wilmer herself. The pair were allegedly seen together at LA nightspot Avalon. Another story suggested that Ashlee had taken a 30-mile drive out of LA to meet up with Wilmer on the desert set of his movie *La Muerto*. After hugging and holding hands, they disappeared to Wilmer's trailer for a late-night snack of burgers and fries. 'There was no kissing but are they more than just buddies?' asked one source.

Although friends of Ashlee insisted the relationship with Wilmer was purely platonic, Lindsay was still upset by even the suggestion that anything had happened. Lindsay and Wilmer still had plenty of unresolved business to deal with. Despite their claims to the contrary, a friendship had never really taken off. Whenever the former sweethearts chanced upon each other in a club, sparks would automatically fly. Subsequently, they would try to avoid each other, often taking cover at different ends of a crowded room. Occasionally, however, they would both succumb to heated emotion. Unfortunately for Lindsay, one such instance was heavily documented in the press.

Lindsay and a group of friends had arranged to meet at trendy New York club Suede for the evening. It was one of Lindsay's favourite haunts and she had a lot of friends in tow. Looking immaculate as ever, she sashayed across the dance floor to a private booth where a gaggle of girlfriends was waiting. Out of the corner of her eye, however, Lindsay caught sight of a deeply tanned guy with chiselled features that unmistakably belonged to Wilmer. Sipping tentatively on an energy drink, she couldn't help but look over from her booth. Locked in an intense gaze, both parties stood up and moved to the dance floor. Without saying a word, they threw down moves in a dance-off.

Bystanders were both amazed and highly amused. 'They were dancing on top of the banquettes, and then Wilmer does this almost Michael Jackson impression on the dance floor!' a source later revealed. 'It was like a scene out of a comedy movie. It was really, really funny. The whole crowd was just staring at them.'

According to later reports, Pamela Anderson, Stephen Dorff and JC Chasez were among those watching in disbelief. Glancing at each other momentarily, the pair would dance even harder. As the track ended, the couple parted without saying a word to each other.

Could it have been a mirror image of the incident in which Britney and Justin allegedly duelled with fancy footwork in an LA club back in March 2002?

On top of all this Lindsay was once again admitted to hospital. This time she was suffering from chest pains. After giving her sinus and chest X-rays, the doctors diagnosed Lindsay to be suffering from a bout of bronchitis. Her publicist confirmed, 'Lindsay has been under the weather.'

Finally, no traumatic period in Lindsay's life would be complete without the involvement of her father. After spending the Christmas period in a rehabilitation centre, Michael Lohan had supposedly emerged a new man. He publicly thanked both God and his family for helping him in his 'darkest hour'. 'The judge's order to me to enter rehab was actually the best Christmas present I could have had,' he proclaimed, though not everyone was convinced by his remarks. 'When I come out, I want to do a project for rehab and donate to the hospitals that helped me,' he continued. He was even considering filming a reality-TV show about the rehab centre, he would later say.

Despite turning over a new leaf, he refused to admit he had ever been a victim of drug dependency. 'When I came here, I had no chemical dependency. I was checked and had zero, zero, zero.' Instead, his problems stemmed from underlying anger-management issues. 'Paxil is amazing,' he said of the anti-depressant. 'It's a wonder drug.'

Michael saw the New Year as an opportunity to change his ways and start a new life. 'Look, all I can say is, God knows what's in my heart and He'll take care of me. He knows I don't mean harm. My wife, Dina, is a very good person. The truth is, she's said four or five times she'd divorce me, but she hasn't. She knows I love her. And I love my family. My daughter Lindsay said she loves me. And they can't keep my family away from me. When I come home and go to court, I'll tell Dina, "Whatever you want. You want to reconcile, divorce, whatever you want, I'll do." I'm just praying to God.'

Unfortunately – but somewhat unsurprisingly – these resolutions were short-lived. Michael had promised to give Dina whatever she wanted, but what she wanted was a divorce. On 18 January 2006, she slapped him with the appropriate papers. Alleging her estranged husband was a philanderer who frequently abused her, she was suing him for alimony, full custody of the children and $1 million in damages.

Fed up with the constant arguing between her

parents, Lindsay fully supported her mother's decision. 'Dina believes for the good of her family and, hopefully, Michael's long-term goal of sobriety that the end of this marriage should happen quickly and painlessly,' Lindsay's publicist Leslie Sloane Zelnik told the press. Dina had made her decision; she wanted to close this chapter of her life for good. 'I want this to move quickly. I wish him the best and I just want to move on.'

But, when court papers were leaked to the press, some extremely dramatic revelations were made. According to the documents, Michael Lohan had told the family security guard of a plan he'd devised to kill his wife and children. 'OJ Simpson has nothing on me!' he allegedly boasted. 'I know exactly how I'm going to kill [them]. I know when I'm going to do it and I'm going to enjoy it.'

The documents went on to allege he'd made previous death threats in 2003. He had allegedly told family friends that, if he ever caught 'Dina with another man, OJ Simpson will have nothing on me'.

The list of accusations read like a shocking soap-opera storyline. In May 2004, Dina accused Michael of throwing her down the stairs and slamming her arm into a door before forcing her into a basement where he allegedly sodomised her against her will. At the time, however, no police report was filed.

Two months later, he allegedly threw himself on

the driveway in front of his wife's car and screamed at their two youngest children, 'If Mommy leaves Daddy, I'm going to hang myself in the garage.'

In March 2004, Dina claimed he 'violently seized' the children's miniature Yorkshire terrier, shoved it into a cage and kicked it across the floor.

The reports also claimed Michael had made a nuisance of himself at several of Lindsay's public appearances. He allegedly followed Lindsay and her family to a press junket in Los Angeles in April 2004 and caused a scene at the Four Seasons Hotel by chasing one child out of the room and terrifying Lindsay's publicist, who took cover in a cupboard. 'If you don't get your mother to ride in the fucking car with me, I'm going to kill her!' he apparently screamed at one frightened child.

The papers also claimed that, in September 2004, during a meeting between Dina and executives from Lindsay's record label, Michael followed her to the restaurant Cipriani and yelled that his wife was a 'whore' and a 'slut'.

The leaked documents shocked and repelled the public. The allegations were deplorable. But the accusations went back even further, to the days when Lindsay was just a child. In March 2000, two years after Lindsay had appeared in *The Parent Trap*, her father allegedly choked his sleeping wife and, during a June 2002 family holiday at the

Fontainebleu Hilton, he was also accused of hitting his wife.

Dina was further quoted in the court papers as saying, 'He has struck me while I was holding the baby [Lindsay's brother Michael] and has broken a glass table while the baby was crawling around the living room. In addition, he threw a carriage across the room in the direction of the baby in an attempt to strike me.'

Dina's lawyer also claimed that Michael once threatened to kill Dina after she had him arrested for beating her on the day of their first wedding anniversary. 'He made five life-threatening telephone calls to Dina, threatening to kill her and her father,' she claimed, adding that, three years later, Michael slit his wrists and said he'd commit suicide if Dina divorced him.

Almost verging on the ridiculous, the whole episode grew even more horrific by the day. Lindsay was humiliated to hear her private family problems being discussed in public but, sadly, it was something she'd come to expect. Seeking support in this time of family crisis, Dina and the children joined Lindsay on set for several days. While Lindsay and her mother declined to comment on the divorce papers, preferring to keep a low profile, Michael Lohan couldn't help but land himself in more trouble.

On 19 February 2005, he was arrested in Long

Island and charged with driving while intoxicated and without a licence following a severe car crash. Michael had driven his car off the road, crashed it into a utility pole and miraculously emerged unscathed. Minutes later, the vehicle burst into flames. He was held on a bond of $40,000 and, when lawyers pleaded for the sum to be reduced, the judge simply replied, 'With this long history, I'll leave things the way they are.'

Distraught at the collapse of her son's family, Lindsay's paternal grandmother Marilyn Lohan chose to intervene. She publicly pleaded with Lindsay to patch up differences with her dad, saying, 'I know your father has problems, but it should be separate from your relationship. Just help your father, Lindsay. He loves you – please be there for him.'

Michael conducted several press interviews, each time denying allegations that he'd threatened his wife. He also insisted that he would never harm his children. But any chance of reconciliation with his daughter in the near future was ruined when Michael appeared on TV show *Primetime Live*. Desperate to protect her children, Dina had unsuccessfully attempted to place a gagging order on her husband. 'It's been a nightmare for the children,' pleaded her lawyer. But the judge rejected her appeal on the grounds Michael had also been devastated by the leaked divorce papers.

Michael used the interview to deny he was ruining Lindsay's career. Quite the contrary, the 44-year-old claimed the sensational headlines had helped his daughter's profile. 'She's got more offers than ever now,' he boasted. 'Don't they say any publicity is good publicity? People don't want the good things, they want the dirt.'

But, while his comments might have upset Lindsay, they were nothing compared to what would happen next. No matter what, Michael seemed destined to remain in the public eye.

15

LIFE THROUGH
A LENS

Michael was always full of extravagant business ideas and many journalists even described him as charismatic. Michael had lost his lost his role as respected patriarch and he now wanted to speak to the press, who were more than willing to listen. Despite constantly complaining about the tabloids, Michael frequently sought interviews and TV appearances. He even kept a collection of press clippings. While in rehab, he'd mulled over the idea of a TV show in which press allegations made against celebrities would be investigated and the truth revealed. Although there was great talk, *The Lowdown* (as his work in progress was named) never actually materialised. But then Michael struck upon a new idea, a reality-TV show involving his family.

'We, as a family, have been offered a deal with one of the biggest production companies in reality TV,' he told one newspaper. 'It's a multi-multi-multimillion-dollar deal.'

Living with the Lohans: Over, or Starting Over would follow Dina and Michael as they worked through their divorce. His treatment read, 'Join the Lohans as they invite you into their home, their lives, at work, play and even through their personal trials, as they go through what could be one of this decade's most high-profile and controversial celebrity divorces.' Michael even appeared on *Primetime Live* to promote his proposed show.

Michael stated that a family reunion was his sole motivation for the show – 'It's not about the money... it's about showing both sides of the coin.' He also announced his intention to sue Dina for a portion of his daughter's earnings. He estimated Lindsay was earning up to $40 million a year and he believed he was entitled to $3 million. He argued that he was after his wife's cut, not Lindsay's money. After all, he'd watched so many other 'parasites' live off her career. He also described Lindsay and Dina as 'emotionally unsound' and demanded they submit to alcohol and drug testing.

Lindsay's lawyers responded with a seven-page cease and desist letter sent to news outlets across the country, warning them against publishing any aspects of Michael Lohan's accounts. For legal reasons, Dina couldn't comment on her husband's behaviour, confining herself to observing, 'A lot of what makes Michael Lohan tick is money.'

Lindsay's grandmother (Michael's mother) was selling photos and videotapes of Lindsay as a child. A source was quoted in the *New York Post* saying, 'Michael isn't making any money so his mother is now selling video and photos of Lindsay as a child. It's disgusting.'

A representative for Lindsay sadly confirmed the story. 'Lindsay's grandmother has been nothing but unsupportive of Dina and the children.'

Determined to move on with her life, Lindsay had requested not to be informed of Michael's outcries in the press. She didn't need any more disruptions to her work. She was having enough trouble refuting press stories of her alleged party lifestyle. 'But I did hear that my dad was suing me for alimony,' she remarked incredulously to one magazine before bursting into laughter. 'I'm, like, I was never married to you! So what is it for, abandonment?'

All jokes aside, Lindsay was adamant Michael would not be seeing a cent of the money her mother had rightfully earned. 'He didn't do anything for my career, except go out and not come home at night and make my mom and me stay up and wonder where he was and then show up three days later,' she blasted. 'So

I don't think he deserves anything. He doesn't even deserve my respect.' As for the ridiculous notion that she might agree to a reality-TV show, Lindsay shrugged, 'Whatever... as sick as it sounds, a reality show might help, actually. At least then people could get to the truth.'

However much Lindsay tried, her father's forays into the media were difficult to ignore. While Dina and her publicist reassured the press that Lindsay was 'doing just fine', in truth the situation had hurt her deeply.

There were very few people left on whom Lindsay Lohan could rely. In April 2005, while Lindsay was away filming in New York, burglars ransacked her LA home, stealing more than $10,000 worth of electronic equipment. Lindsay had taken great care to lock her apartment when she'd left. She'd even asked friends to keep a watchful eye on the place. With state-of-the-art locks how could someone break in without her secret passcode?

Lindsay grew convinced people were stealing from her on a regular basis. 'I've been marking my money lately because I had a friend who was stealing from me.' Lindsay had already ended several close friendships over an issue of trust. 'Sometimes, I'll tell people in my life something completely out of this world – that could never be true – and then I'll see it in the tabloids. That's how you find out who you can trust,' she explained, obviously saddened by the need for such extreme measures.

While press stories had emotionally injured Lindsay on a number of occasions, very soon the paparazzi were posing a physical threat. Now familiar with her Hollywood lifestyle, Lindsay was accustomed to photographers lurking at every street corner. Resigned to the fact most of them would refuse to leave her alone, she attempted to co-operate in the hope that they would strike a deal. 'It's the price you pay,' she sighed. 'The more you run from them and hide, the more they want to take your picture.'

She criticised other stars who constantly complained about harassment from the press. What good would that ever do? She was referring specifically to an incident involving Justin Timberlake and Cameron Diaz. The couple had stolen a photographer's camera after they alleged that he had jumped out on them from behind a bush and provoked a fight. 'I mean, you have Cameron Diaz and Justin Timberlake hitting people now… It gets frustrating but you have to understand that's their job and they're just trying to get a picture. It's a blessing rather than something you should hate… If you let them take a picture, it's a little bit easier.'

On a number of occasions, Lindsay had agreed to pose for a shot on the condition that they would leave her in peace afterwards. But frequently the press failed to keep their side of the bargain. 'That's when it gets crazy... suddenly, there are ten of them!' Often, photographers would chase Lindsay's car around the LA streets.

On one occasion, a photographer's minivan crashed into her Mercedes Benz. Lindsay recalls the incident in great detail. 'I had my friend in the car and it happened so fast. I couldn't get out the side door, which had jammed shut, and I knew a story of someone that was close to one of my family members that passed away in their car, because someone hit their door and then they couldn't get out of it. So all I could think at that moment was: "I can't get outta my door, I'm gonna die in this car, my door's jammed!" Then my friend, who had just whacked her head on the window, was panicking because she couldn't find the unlock switch, so what was going on was incredible.'

When Lindsay finally did break herself free from the vehicle, she was shocked to find photographers were still taking her picture. 'I said, "What are you doing?" I was in shock; I did not know what to do.'

Speaking after the event, Lindsay was simply relieved no one had been hurt. She was also glad her younger sister Ali hadn't been in the passenger seat. Too young to know better, she loved all the attention and would often 'poke her head out of the window and smile'. All Lindsay really had to contend with was a few bruises. 'I'm sore in the neck. It was pretty scary. I didn't expect anything to happen. I turned my head to talk to my friend and got rammed in the side.'

But the incident did raise an important issue about the increasing threat paparazzi photographers were posing to celebrities. The 24-year-old photographer who had pursued Lindsay was booked on suspicion of assault with a deadly weapon and released on $35,000 bail. Although he was never actually charged, the case did prompt California's film-star governor Arnold Schwarzenegger to pass a new law allowing celebrities to collect large damages awards from paparazzi who harass them. Lindsay's accident was just one of many. More recently, Reese Witherspoon had been chased off the road by a group of photographers and, a month later, Scarlett Johannson would suffer a similar fate.

Soon after the accident, Lindsay was back at work. In many ways, her busy schedule was a welcome distraction from all the other problems she had to deal with. Besides, one of her forthcoming engagements would involve more pleasure than pain – Lindsay was due to appear at the 2005 MTV Awards. *Mean Girls* had been nominated for awards in several categories and it looked likely to sweep the board. Lindsay couldn't wait! She was up for Best Actress and, although she didn't want to tempt fate, she knew there was a good chance she might win.

Preparing a speech was tough… but finding an outfit was even harder! When Lindsay arrived at the Shrine Auditorium in LA, she was blinded by flashbulbs. Smiling sweetly, she took time to sign a couple of autographs for fans before moving inside. Journalists were firing questions at her from behind a roped-off area. Today's topic of conversation appeared to be her recent altercation with the paparazzi. She declined to comment.

Once inside, Lindsay took time to kick back and catch up with friends she hadn't seen in some time. When the time for the award announcements came, Lindsay felt nervous. Her *Mean Girls* co-stars assured her she had nothing to worry about. Samuel L Jackson was presenting the award for Best Film Female. Lindsay had always admired his work; she was so busy trying to recall all the movies he'd starred in she almost didn't hear her name being read out!

Screaming, she rushed on stage to collect her award. But an even greater honour was to follow. As the pair were walking on stage, Lindsay's hero revealed he was, in fact, a fan of her work as well. 'I've seen your movie *Mean Girls* about five times and I love it!' he confessed.

Lindsay couldn't believe her ears. 'Not only is it amazing to hear that from you, but it's so nice to hear that from someone, because all you read is: "Lindsay is out 'til four in the morning partying, da, da, da, da,"' Lindsay replied.

The *Pulp Fiction* star went on to ask Lindsay if she'd fully recovered from her accident. Unlike the gaggle of reporters outside, he seemed to be genuinely concerned.

In celebration of the MTV Awards, Lindsay had organised her own after-show party at swanky bar The Standard. 'I threw a little gathering of about a hundred people,' she recalls. 'It was very small but really cool. Chris Rock was there and Quentin Tarantino, most of the people from [*Herbie*]. It was really cool. It was fun and it was controlled. It was relaxing.'

Oddly, that didn't seem the case when a raspy Lindsay Lohan appeared on TV the next day. 'I kind of lost my voice a little bit,' she confessed. 'I was the host of the party and that was a bit stressful. I was running around all night trying to make people feel comfortable.'

But, while the press could find nothing to write about inside the party, there was plenty of chaos outdoors. When Ashlee Simpson and her sister Jessica arrived at the party, they were stunned to discover that their names could not be found on the guest list. Responding graciously and not wishing to cause a scene, the Simpson sisters departed to Jimmy Fallon's party at the Argyle Hotel instead.

Lindsay later explained there had been a mistake

with both names mislaid on the list. A spokesperson for the Simpsons added, 'Ashlee and Jessica had a great time at Jimmy's party, which was the hottest one of the night.'

The press refused to give up that easily, though. With Hilary out of the picture, they needed a new rival to pitch Lindsay against. Both girls would grow tired of the allegations. 'She's a sweet girl, but we're obviously not best friends,' Ashlee told one magazine. 'I don't see her all the time, but when we do see each other we always say hi.'

In turn, Lindsay complimented Jessica for always looking fantastic. 'I'll never look as good as Jessica Simpson, who always looks perfect.'

After the hype surrounding her MTV party had calmed down, Lindsay had time to reflect on her earlier car crash. To her credit, she'd handled the situation with calm. Although she didn't necessarily like it, she understood the press were simply doing their job. But she did disagree with their methods. 'It's not safe and it's not fair what they do to people.'

But she wasn't so willing to forgive when a similar incident occurred a few months later. A group of 20 photographers had been waiting for Lindsay outside The Ivy restaurant and followed her as she left. While trying to escape, however, she collided with another vehicle making an illegal U-turn. At the time, Lindsay was travelling with her publicist. 'My first instinct was: "Get out of this car – they're going to start taking pictures,'" Lindsay told reporters.

Fearing the paparazzi would leap out at any moment, she fled into a nearby store called Hideaway House Antiques. 'I mean, the irony of that is just creepy and weird!' she laughed afterwards. Spotting the paparazzi outside, she ran and hid in a corner. 'I sat down on this old chair and I look down and there's blood specks all over the chair!' she recalls. 'I looked at my assistant. I said, "Buy this chair. It's not getting sold on eBay!"'

Much later, however, Lindsay was furious to discover a headlamp from her black Mercedes was up for auction on the internet site. The listing read: 'Friend of mine works at the place where this car was taken. Today is your lucky day, you are bidding on the passenger-side headlight of Lindsay's black Mercedes.'

After the crash occurred, a number of newspaper reports questioned who had been at fault. Victoria Recano, a reporter on the TV show *Insider*, happened to be filming in the area and saw the accident take place. She claimed that Lindsay's car had been 'going really fast'. But police were satisfied that the actress had been well within the speed limit. The following day, television pictures showed the shattered car surrounded by debris with both front airbags deployed.

Although the paparazzi were not directly involved

in this instance, Lindsay's publicist Leslie Sloane Zelnik named them as a contributory factor. 'The first time, it was a paparazzi running into her, and this time she was trying to get away by driving out of the area,' she argued. 'If this doesn't stop, someone's going to get killed.'

The press were turning up the heat on Lindsay, who would be forced to respond accordingly. But, while a few cuts and bruises would heal quickly, very soon their hurtful stories would leave more lasting scars.

16

TWINKLE, TWINKLE, LITTLE STAR

When Lindsay first arrived on the Hollywood scene, one of her greatest qualities had been her down-to-earth normality. Unlike the stick-thin blondes who seemed to proliferate in her neighbourhood, the curvy redhead stood out from the crowd. But, soon, Lindsay came to resent her individuality. Working in a profession where, sadly, looks are everything, she became increasingly conscious about her appearance. As Lindsay's profile started to grow internationally, her waistline began to shrink at an alarmingly similar rate. The press quickly picked up on the dramatic change in physique and Lindsay's weight became the focus of much speculation.

Lindsay started to shed weight after her first visit to hospital back in October 2004. 'When I went to the hospital, I lost a lot of weight, about 20-25 pounds,' she admitted. Worryingly, she was actually pleased with her weight loss and determined to keep it off. 'I'm happy to have lost weight,' she said. 'And I'm working to keep it off.'

Apparently, the whole hospital experience forced the young star to reassess her health. In the past, she'd counted running down 11 flights of stairs in stilettos as a workout. 'I am so lazy. I never stop eating,' she once confessed. 'If I have any time in the day, I will go to the gym. I'll jog and do crunches, and that's it. I feel so great after that. I'm, like, "Yeah, I worked out this month... once!"'

But now she was exercising properly with a trainer. 'While I was filming *Herbie* last year, I got sick because I wasn't taking care of myself. I was eating junk food and not working out and not being healthy.' She claimed her dramatic drop in dress size – from a US 6 to a 2 – was the result of 'eating healthier and working out'.

Ever since she entered the acting business, Lindsay had been painfully aware of the pressures to be thin. It was something she'd often complained about in the past. 'I don't like the fact that people my age are dealing with today's images, because they're not realistic, and people think that's how they should be presenting themselves. It's scary because these little kids are looking at you like you're perfect, and nobody's perfect. People I admire, like Marilyn Monroe and Ann-Margret, had beautiful figures.'

Discussing the same subject in another interview, she said, 'It's definitely harder for girls to like themselves today. They're so concerned about fitting into 25-waist jeans.'

As Lindsay started to shed the pounds, people began complimenting her on her new look. To some extent, that made her even more aware. She recalls a conversation with her record-label boss Tommy Mottola. 'He said to me, "You lost a lot of weight! You look great!"... I'm, like, "Well, was I fat before?"'

She also told David Letterman on his show that she felt a 'pressure to keep it off'. But Lindsay insisted she couldn't be happier. 'Kate Moss is my fashion icon and now I can fit into more clothes and things look better. I lost about 20 pounds, although, compared with a lot of actresses my age, I'm actually overweight.'

In fact, the only drawback Lindsay could find with her new figure was the loss of her boobs. 'I miss my boobs! It sucks!' she laughed. Well, at least she could finally silence gossips on the topic of their authenticity!

Not everyone shared Lindsay's opinion. One group of fans even set up a website – Feedlindsay.com – begging her to put on some weight. Over 3,000 worried admirers signed a petition saying, 'We urge you, Lindsay, to please pick up a sandwich and eat it, or ice cream, or any food that might put those oh-so-cute pounds back on.' The site also sold souvenirs and T-shirts printed with the slogans 'Feed Lindsay' and 'Eat Me'.

Lindsay was neither flattered nor amused by suggestions she should pile on the pounds. She grew tired of frequent remarks about her weight and dismissed concerns that she might be suffering from an eating disorder. 'I was never on a crash diet, because that's not what I do. I could never be one of those girls who throws up after eating. And my mother would kill me if I did anything stupid.'

She even went to great lengths to demonstrate her love of food. 'I always have to eat dessert,' she told one interviewer. 'I am a McDonald's girl. A Big Mac and fries? It just makes me feel happy. I am also really big on Taco Bell, like, I could eat that any time.' Her publicist added, 'She eats as many muffins as she likes.'

But, over time, Lindsay did favour plenty of diet foods. She named her ultimate late-night snack as Tasti D-Lite. 'It tastes like Mister Softee, not frozen yogurt, but it's really low in calories so it doesn't make you feel gross,' she explained. 'I learned about it from *Sex and the City*.'

But the accusations of anorexia continued and Lindsay grew increasingly fed up with having to justify herself. In June, there were even reports that she'd collapsed in a gym. 'I'm not skinny for the wrong reasons,' she declared defiantly. Much to her chagrin, even Lindsay's doctor was querying her weight loss. 'He was like, "Are you anorexic? Are you making yourself throw up? Are drugs involved?" I asked him, "Are you saying this because you've read it in magazines? Because I don't!"'

Instead, Lindsay attributed her new svelte figure to a natural loss of baby fat. 'I do take care of my body – there is nothing to change. I'm really happy,' she sighed. 'I'm growing up in front of the public eye, and people are watching me change. When you watch a child change, you see their bodies, their image, the style of their clothes, everything changes. You mature, it happens!'

In an attempt to detract attention from herself, Lindsay also drew attention to a proliferation of young stars in the industry suffering from eating disorders. 'I'm around girls, even in the movies, that are like, "I don't feel good, I just ate a lot, I'm going to throw up." Like at the *Vanity Fair* photo shoot [for the cover of the July 2003 issue] of all the young stars, no one ate. I was going straight to the pasta, and the other girls were eating salad. And I'm the one people say [has an eating disorder]."

Fed up with her squeaky-clean image, Lindsay caused a mini uproar when she finally admitted to having dabbled with cannabis. In the past, she'd sworn 'scout's honour' that she'd never tried drugs. 'I've never been one to get wasted and experiment with drugs,' she said. But that was the previous year and, obviously, in the interim period something had changed. 'I'm not going to deny the fact that I've tried pot,' she admitted, before quickly adding, 'I hated it.' But, in almost the same breath, she was quick to deny any allegations of cocaine abuse. 'I've never tried cocaine. I've seen my father... I've seen how it messes with families and, you know, it fucks your life up. If I hadn't experienced that, I may have gone a different route, I don't know. But I've seen how it literally tore my parents apart.'

In light of those experiences, Lindsay felt especially sensitive about the issue of drugs. But any attempts to refute claims she'd used them often seemed futile. The press now seemed determined to pin something on her; they were just waiting to pounce. 'The thing is, people get to the point where they're so bloody desperate that they'll say anything. And you really can't do anything about it because the more you defend yourself, the more it looks like you're guilty.'

Lindsay was sick and tired of reiterating that she was now an adult and old enough to be having a social life. 'Everyone thinks I'm this crazy drug addict and I'd like to straighten things out.' She criticised magazines for painting her as 'this party animal – like an old woman who's partied her whole life… I know my limits'.

When Lindsay's father linked the star's dramatic loss of weight to recent family traumas, he wasn't far off the mark. 'People wonder why Lindsay's so thin. It's because of all this garbage between her mother and me. She's beaten up inside… it's ripped our whole family apart,' he said.

Even ex-boyfriend Aaron Carter had some words of support for his former puppy love. 'She's going through a rough time right now, family drama. I've been through the same stuff. It can cause health problems and it can cause mental problems. She's just got to stay strong and she'll get through it. It doesn't mean she has an addiction to drugs, it doesn't mean she is a partygoer. That girl works her butt off, and dealing with all of her family stuff at the same time, it's going to do it to you.'

Over time, it became apparent that Lindsay had a problem; she was getting too thin. Any baby fat she might have had was long gone. She'd crossed over the line of 'healthy' into far more dangerous territory. Gossip magazines now compared her frail and willowy figure to that of her close friend super-waif Nicole Ritchie. Then, in May 2005 when Lindsay was filming *Saturday Night Live*, the situation came to a head.

Given the amount of media attention now focused on Lindsay and her social life, the *SNL* team thought it would be amusing to open the show with a skit on her supposed woes. Happy to poke fun at herself in the name of comedy, Lindsay eagerly agreed to take part. She had nothing to hide, after all. The sketch opens with a monologue from the dangerously thin teen saying, 'If you read the tabloids, they say I'm too skinny, I'm at clubs every night, I'm dating everyone...' Dressed as a rather worse-for-wear Lindsay, Amy Poehler interrupts her by swinging into shot. Echoing the Charles Dickens classic *A Christmas Carol*, 'the ghost of Lindsay future' warns of what will happen if she doesn't stop her partying ways. 'Lindsay, your life is moving too fast, you gotta slow it down,' says the ghost before giving a crystal ball interpretation of the future. 'Let me see, we did *Herbie: Fully Loaded*, *Mean Girls 2* – that was a suck bomb – *National Lampoon's Jamaican Vacation*... we did, like, eight Lifetime movies, and now we host a Cinemax show called *Night Passions*... You're married to Tommy Lee, genius... and, do me a favour, some time in the near future when you're out partying with Nicole Ritchie, do not get this tattoo.' With that, the ghost pulls down her shirt slightly to reveal 'I Love Bo Bice' on one breast and an image of the *American Idol* finalist on the other. Lindsay shrugs, 'Well, I do love me some Bo Bice.'

Although the sketch provoked raucous laughter, it carried darker undertones. Lindsay's sudden drop in dress size had raised alarm among people who cared about her. The bubbly and charismatic actress had become a familiar face on set over the years and many of the crew regarded her as family. Having watched Lindsay almost disappear from view, they were extremely concerned for her health. It was time to intervene and offer advice. Amy Poehler took Lindsay to one side. 'You're too skinny,' she said matter-of-factly. This time she wasn't joking. 'I'm not gonna ask you why, but you're too skinny and I don't like it.'

Recalling the episode clearly, Tina Fey (Lindsay's pal from the *Mean Girls* days) said, 'Amy was good and tough on her. After that, both Tina and *SNL* producer Lorne Michaels took Lindsay aside and spoke to her about eating disorders. Lindsay recalls they sat her down directly before the show and told her, 'You need to take care of yourself. We care about you too much, and we've seen too many people do this, and you're talented.'

Lindsay burst into tears. 'I knew I had a problem and I couldn't admit it... I saw that *SNL* after I did it. My arms were disgusting. I had no arms.' The final straw came when Lindsay saw a shocking picture of herself in *Star* magazine. 'I looked at it and was like, Jesus Christ...' she says. Both her little brothers and sister called up in tears.

Months later in January 2006, Lindsay would publicly confess the whole episode in *Vanity Fair* magazine. 'I would make myself sick,' she confessed to the journalist, indicating she had been suffering from bulimia. But, for now, everyone agreed to keep quiet. Months later, Lindsay would cryptically infer that she'd addressed any eating problems. Although still remarkably thin, she'd at least regained a few pounds. 'I was going through a rough time and I probably wasn't taking care of myself – I wasn't. I want to encourage young girls to not get to that point,' she said.

Instead, Lindsay expected to read headlines suggesting she'd put on too much weight. 'Now they're going to say I am overweight, which is ridiculous. I don't know what to say to that… you grow up and you mature.'

When later quizzed by *Vanity Fair* about Lindsay's weight issues, Dina remained blasé, quickly glossing over any problems. 'It happens to people in different periods of their life,' she sighed. 'She took it a little far, maybe, and pulled back quickly and is fine.' She argued that people were being overly dramatic, making Lindsay lose all perspective. '[It] made Lindsay think it was more magnified. She was 19 looking at it. I'm 43 looking at it – it wasn't as bad as it looked.' She even suggested magazines had digitally manipulated Lindsay's arms to make them look thinner.

Whether Lindsay's problems had been exaggerated or not, she'd at least chosen to address them. It marked an important turning point in the young adult's life; she was starting to accept responsibility for her actions – she was growing up. Coinciding with her mature outlook on life, Lindsay was also beginning to land more meaty film roles. She'd already switched to CAA (Creative Artists Agency in California) in a bid to secure more adult scripts. Her opportunity came when respected director Robert Altman (responsible for cult military black comedy *M*A*S*H*) invited Lindsay to join the cast of *A Prairie Home Companion*. She would play Meryl Streep's daughter alongside a star-studded cast of Lily Tomlin, Kevin Kline and Garrison Keillor.

Lindsay was ecstatic; the offer came as a great honour. 'It's going to be so cool,' she gushed, with pre-production excitement. 'I'm a big fan of Meryl Streep. I mean, come on, she's so terrific and I have so much to learn from her. Believe me, I'm going to be watching her like a hawk, just to see how she prepares and everything.'

In preparation for her new role, Lindsay underwent another dramatic change – she dyed her famous red locks blonde. Combined with her new weight loss, people commented that she looked a completely different person. Lindsay joked that the new hair colour actually gave her the excuse to make more ditzy comments. Ever since she was a child, she'd desperately wanted blonde hair like her mother.

'I look like my mom,' she said, admiring herself with a compact mirror. 'My mom's amazing – and she's beautiful!' Fortunately, Lindsay wasn't about to ditch her red locks just yet. 'But I love my red hair. It makes me spunkier.'

On the first day of shooting in Minnesota, Lindsay was scared. Robert Altman was famous for his unorthodox methods of filming and he would often encourage actors to improvise in scenes; some were up to 25 pages long. One scene involved Lindsay singing *a capella* along with Meryl Streep and Lily Tomlin.

In the film, Lindsay has no father. When the women began singing about her absent dad, Lindsay broke down and started to cry. The cameras continued rolling and very soon tears were streaming from Meryl and Lily. Altman was impressed by Lindsay's performance. 'She was excellent,' he said.

Crew members congratulated her, saying, 'That was amazing, I can't believe it wasn't scripted.'

'They were so nice to me and kind,' recalls Lindsay. 'I was so proud of myself. That changed me a lot.'

According to magazine reports, Meryl Streep even offered to mentor Lindsay after the pair became close on set. 'Lindsay's been told Meryl offered to mentor her and she should take advantage of it,' said an undisclosed source. 'But Lindsay is just like, "Oh, she probably doesn't want to deal with me." I think she's just a little starstruck. Lindsay's just so in awe of Meryl.'

After a great deal of reflection and heartache, Lindsay was now ready to straighten out her personal life. Even more than ever, she was determined to focus on her career. In order to move forward, she understood there were many loose ends she still needed to tie up. Unfortunately, one of those was her father.

In June, he'd been sentenced to 21 months in prison for offences committed over the previous seven months. Although out of sight, he was never out of Lindsay's mind. Problems resurfaced while Lindsay was promoting *Herbie*. On set, she could find escapism from her troubles, seeking refuge in another character, but, placed under public scrutiny, she felt nervous and exposed.

The first dramatic instance occurred during the US première screening of *Herbie* at the El Capitan Theater in Hollywood. Lindsay stormed out of the theatre after discovering a track she'd recorded for the project had been moved to the closing credits. Lindsay had worked extremely hard to record the song to fit with the film production schedule. Now it appeared her efforts had been wasted. 'I pushed myself to get it done for the movie when I probably should have waited,' she sighed.

Lindsay often blamed her frail emotions on an

obsession with work. 'I'm very strong willed and it's very easy for me to say no. I have a somewhat addictive personality. Also, when someone really irritates me, I have a very short-term temper. I really have no patience. My dad is a workaholic – and that's how I am.'

Ironically, Lindsay's commitment to her career was called into question once again when she cancelled a series of promotional engagements in Europe. Journalists pointed out that, while Lindsay had been fully capable of partying with friends, the following morning she was mysteriously unable to work. In reality, nothing could be further from the truth. Struggling to deal with her parents' bitter divorce, Lindsay could no longer wear a brave face in public.

It was around this time that Lindsay started writing 'Confessions of a Broken Heart (Daughter to Father)', a song dedicated to her father. While penning lyrics in her hotel room, she suddenly broke down and started crying. She rushed to her publicist's room and, without thinking, began dialling the number for the Nassau County Jail. 'My father's in there – you need to put me on the phone with him!' she screamed at the guard. 'This is not right. I'm Lindsay Lohan, Michael Lohan's daughter.' Afraid the guard might leak something to the press, Leslie Sloane Zelnik tried to stop Lindsay, but with little success.

Lindsay never did reach her father, but it was

already clear in her mind that she needed to come home. 'I'm coming home,' she said in a phone call to her brother Michael. 'I'm quitting this press tour. I don't care if I never work again. I need to be with my family.'

The remaining cast members continued with the tour and Lindsay's director, Angela Robinson, wished her the best of luck. 'She's having some troubles at home,' the sympathetic director told journalists. 'She wanted to go back and deal with her family, because she had some personal stuff going on, so we definitely miss her here, but I think it's best that she do that.'

With hindsight, Lindsay regrets her actions as irresponsible. But, at the time, she had no choice in the matter. The decision marked an important turning point in her life. Having remained silent for so long, Lindsay was now ready to express the inner turmoil she'd kept locked inside. It was finally time to communicate with her father.

17

STRAIGHT FROM
THE HEART

Assistants and technicians are huddled closely around a TV monitor. 'She looks fabulous,' coos one make-up artist.

'I think we should cut earlier,' says an engineer. 'Or maybe do that shot again. What do you think, Lindsay?' he says to the director of today's shoot.

The scene in question is a sequence from Lindsay's 'Confessions of a Broken Heart' video. Dealing with subject matter so close to home, for once Miss Lohan is calling the shots. It was actually Tommy Mottola who suggested that she should direct the video. It made perfect sense. When she initially approached him about recording the song, he agreed on one condition – that she take full creative control. '[She has] complete knowledge of the medium [and] even a greater understanding of the material,' he gushed. 'Lindsay is one of the most talented, creative and intuitive people I've ever met.' Tommy also referred to 'Confessions' as 'one of the best I've heard in my career'.

Lindsay agreed that directing the video for 'Confessions' would be the perfect opportunity to set the record straight on her much maligned family life. 'People have so many opinions of me. I wanted to show my vision of how everything has taken place and the truth of what happened. I can do that through directing this video.'

Lindsay was nervous about making her directorial début, but Tommy had complete faith in her ability. He assured the modest star she was ready and that he'd lend her all the support she needed.

The video shoot takes place in Chelsea, New York. Lindsay has chosen to shoot the entire video in a shop window, attracting plenty of curious passers-by. '[The video is set] in a storefront, on display, because my life is on display,' she says. The set is a replica of Lindsay's home in Merrick, Long Island. Her bedroom is pink and adorned with posters of puppies. Lindsay and her sister Ali will play themselves, while actors will play her parents. The video depicts Michael Lohan arriving home to find Dina reading a magazine in the living room. The TV set is blaring in the background and a report detailing Michael's latest arrest for drunk-driving flashes across the screen. He knocks Dina to the floor in anger and drags her across the room. The fight creates quite a stir on the street outside. Even the police arrive to disperse crowds. Ali is cowering in the bedroom with her hands clasped firmly over her ears. She's dressed in a tutu having just returned from a ballet lesson. Meanwhile, Lindsay hides in the bathroom writing lyrics to the song. She thrashes around the room sobbing, 'Daughter to father! Daughter to father! Tell me the truth... did you ever love me?' She's wearing a rather extravagant Monique Lhuillier gown, somewhat at odds with a scene of domestic violence. She says it's to signify that she's 'all dressed up [with] nowhere to go'. She continues, 'I wanted to do something that was kind of extravagant up top so, when we go back and edit, I can catch the light and sparkle.' Emotionally drained, Lindsay takes a cigarette break in her trailer.

She admitted the scenes were difficult to record and she had to stop herself from doing any additional takes. 'I cried as I watched. Watching my sister in the scenes, I cried. When we filmed the argument between the parents, that made me cry.' But the video did function as a form of therapy. 'It's like the best acting that I've ever been able to do is in this video. I freak out and just kinda go with it and create my own scene.'

The finished product actually proved too hardcore for MTV. 'We had to tone it down a drop – which is saying something!' admits Tommy Mottola.

Whereas in the past Lindsay may have worried about offending younger fans, she no longer believed such precautions were necessary. 'It's offensive and I want it to be. I'm saying Dad's what I needed... I was seeking your comfort and I didn't have it.'

At first, Dina was sceptical about allowing Ali to appear in the video, but the aspiring child star was desperate to join her big sister on screen. Ali explained that she needed to express her own feelings towards her dad. 'Michael was in and out of jail during my marriage, so it was really me on my own with my parents,' said Dina. 'Ali was really young but she wanted to tell her side because she was angry that he [Michael] did this and embarrassed her. All the kids at school would say, "We just saw your dad on the news." I mean, he never thought of that.'

Ali was thrilled at an opportunity to take part in the video. She loved every minute of it, although it did bring back bad memories. Lindsay also enjoyed directing her younger sister, whom she's referred to in the past as being like 'a daughter'. 'I like being able to teach her things at a young age and it's therapy for her as well. We've been through a lot thus far in our lives together, and to share that experience with someone I love and care for so much was amazing.'

Lindsay and her younger sister have always shared a very close relationship. In the absence of a stable father figure, Lindsay had tried desperately hard to compensate by lavishing attention on Aliana. Lindsay was extremely protective of her sister and tried to stand up for her wherever possible. Having a father in jail and a sister in Hollywood made Ali an easy target for bullies in the school playground. Lindsay understood from her own experience just how cruel jealous young girls could be.

One day, Lindsay arrived home to find her sister in tears. It transpired that a girl at school had been giving her a hard time. Lindsay was incensed. 'I got the little girl's number and I was going to call and say something,' recalls Lindsay. Shaking with anger, she dialled the number. Ali leaned over and grabbed the receiver. 'I can handle it,' she said firmly. Perhaps it was better to let her little sister fight her own battles.

Throughout Lindsay's whole career, Ali had functioned as a barometer for any decision Lindsay made. 'I always ask her what she and her friends think,' Lindsay had confessed in the past. '"Ali, do you like this outfit?" "No, that looks slutty." "Ali, do you like this one?" "Yes, you look really pretty." Then when she's mad at me: "Lindsay, you have fat thighs."'

More than anything, Lindsay couldn't believe the rate at which her little sister was growing up. The seven-year gap between the pair had always seemed a lifetime, but now it was closing in quickly. 'My sister is just hysterical,' Lindsay told one magazine. 'One night, my mom was out to dinner, and I couldn't get in touch with her. So I called home and said, "Ali, where's Mom? Do you know when she's coming back?" Ali said, "No." I said, "Ali, it's midnight... why are you still awake?" She said, "I'm hanging out with my friend watching TV – what's your problem? Mommy's a big girl... she can do whatever she wants and be out late, so snap-snap, girlfriend, and get over it!" The things she says! It's like she's 25. She'll be so mad when she reads that, but she'll love it.'

Watching Ali mature into a young woman, Lindsay recognised elements of her own character. Ali was besotted with her sister and desperate to follow in her famous footsteps. Having signed up to her own agent, she'd already made several appearances alongside Lindsay. She was extremely territorial and couldn't bear the idea of another young star featuring alongside Lindsay. When a cameo role for a young girl came up in *Just My Luck*, Ali was adamant it should be hers. Unfortunately, the directors were after someone Hispanic. 'I wanna meet the director!' Ali demanded to Lindsay, stamping her foot. 'I should be able to do this. I don't want you working with another girl!' Covered in bronzer, Ali read for the part. Lindsay cracks up at the memory. Needless to say, she didn't get the part.

Thanks to her sister, Lindsay had an intimate understanding of her younger audience. She hoped her video would send out a positive message to other young victims of domestic violence. 'It was really to let girls, boys, anyone that's in an abusive relationship, anyone who is going through things like that… to put it out there that it's OK to express how you feel. If I'm in the position where I can take a stand and say something important, then I'd like to do that.'

In many ways, Lindsay felt she had a responsibility to stand up and make a statement. 'We barely have any heroes in this generation,' she complained. 'We look to our musicians from a different time. John Lennon was a man who was able to influence people to believe in peace and recognise things that people are afraid to see for themselves. With the position that actors, singers, ones like me are in, we have not only an obligation, but a chance to make a difference, and have a huge impact on making a difference.'

Only recently, Lindsay had been invited by a friend to attend a Rolling Stones gig. She was now at a stage where she wanted to learn new things and was always eager to hear any musical recommendations. It was the same approach she'd adopted in her acting career and it certainly hadn't done her any harm whatsoever. Listening and observing had always been Lindsay's preferred method of education.

The Stones gig had a huge effect on the impressionable artist. 'Just being a part of something that is so raw and seeing real music happen with amazing artists is an honour and a wonderful thing to be able to do,' she enthused.

Hip-hop producer-turned-superstar Kanye West was another artist Lindsay found inspirational. 'Kanye West is another artist who is not afraid to speak his mind and put what he believes out into the world,' she said with admiration. 'I respect that. Whatever your belief is... there is always someone out there who may and does have the same feelings to some extent – so why not express it?'

One person Lindsay desperately hoped her message would reach was her father. As it happened, he was thrilled to discover her song wasn't an outright character assassination, but simply a sad appeal for a child to be loved by their parent. 'Not a day goes by that I don't think about the words to your song... They've been reminders to me to examine my conscience and re-evaluate my life,' he wrote in an open letter to her through *Vanity Fair*.

In another letter to the *New York Daily News*, he wrote, 'While I always considered and expressed how truly blessed Lindsay as well as my other children are, I never realised how blessed I am to have a daughter as amazing as Lindsay. Hold on to my shirt, honey... soon enough you'll be able to hold on to me! While the media and press love to cover Lindsay enjoying her life and successes, hopefully now they will cover the kind of heart this beautiful and gifted young lady really has.'

Michael was so touched he even composed a musical response of his own. The lyrics were published in the *NYDN* and included the lines 'I loved and protected you, I was there through it all/I do admit, I did at times fall/But these things you know were due to them/The ones that want to have a piece of my gem!'

Lindsay had been anxious about her father's reaction. 'I hope he'll see what I say in the song is "I love you" so many times, that I need him and the crazy things in my life,' she said. 'I hope he sees the positive side of the video rather than the negative. The video is kind of offensive, but it is very raw.'

The process of writing and recording 'Confessions' had obviously helped Lindsay work through a number of issues. Her feelings towards her father were still mixed. 'I love him,' she said assuredly. 'I hope he can get to a good place. I've gone through everything and more that someone could have gone through at my age. I've lived a lifetime already. He needs to focus on what's important to him. The way people act sometimes can be irrational. He needs to find that spiritual common ground with other people.' As for whether she could ever forgive him, she laughed,

'Well, I wouldn't be here without my mother and my father… And I need someone to walk me down the aisle when I get married.'

Now at an important juncture in her life, Lindsay felt it was definitely time to grow. In many ways, she could carry her younger fans along with her. It was time to show the world Lindsay Lohan was growing into a young woman. Lindsay's co-writer and the executive producer of her album, Kara DioGuardi, agreed her new album *A Little More Personal (Raw)* reflected the more mature choices Lindsay was making in her life and work.

Among her upcoming projects were films about the assassinations of Robert Kennedy (*Bobby*, playing opposite Elijah Wood) and John Lennon (*Chapter 27*). Both were assassination stories. 'There were songs on the album that were deeper, with more in-depth focus to her life,' Kara DioGuardi said. 'I think the need to define herself as a young woman as opposed to a young child is becoming more and more evident.'

Lindsay had always turned to songwriting as a form of therapy. She had found that writing lyrics was often the only way to vent her frustrations. The past year had been tough, but it had provided her with plenty of solid material for an album that spoke directly from her heart. No matter how long or arduous her day had been, Lindsay would always set aside some time before bed to scribble observations in her journals. Often, within those words lay the potential for a song. 'There's been a lot going on [in my life lately], and I think people can find that escape in hobbies that they do. I don't do yoga or anything, but some people use that. Everyone has their own thing, and I use writing.'

Whenever Lindsay wanted to escape the mayhem of her everyday world, she would take refuge in the studio. 'When you get into the studio, everything just comes out,' she said. 'All your creative juices are there. I don't [want to] leave. I'll still be in there until all hours, and it's nice to be able to do that.'

But, just like her carefully calculated choice of movie roles, Lindsay knew it was important not to forget her younger fans. 'I do still have the younger fan base and I want them to be able to relate to some lighter songs, but I want to grow with my fans, and I've been trying to do that for so long. I've just grown up really fast, and I'm thankful for that.'

Among the material on her album, Lindsay had chosen to address her difficult break-up with Wilmer. In the song "Black Hole', she sings about finding love letters from an ex. When *TRL* host Vanessa Minillo asked Lindsay whether the account was fictional or a reference to her former beau, the coy actress squirmed uncomfortably. 'Dammit! A little bit of both. I mean, I incorporate everything.' Pressed for even more information, she rolled her eyes. 'It's an ex so it's already [past],' before grudgingly adding, 'Obviously some of it was from Wilmer. Fine.'

After a turbulent year, the Lohan family were confident that their troubles would soon be at an end. In December 2005, Dina and Michael finally opted for a legal separation rather than a divorce. Although the terms of the agreement were undisclosed, Dina was reportedly pleased with the outcome. 'Dina and the children are delighted that this chapter in their lives is finally over. And it *is* over,' said their lawyer.

Michael, meanwhile, was in the midst of a spiritual epiphany and claimed to have found God. 'I want to go into a ministry to learn more about what connects people to their spirituality,' he told TV show *A Current Affair* in an interview from prison. 'I'd like to actually get into homeless shelters or a spiritual rehab or things of that nature that will help people get out of the rut they're in and turn their life and their will over to God instead of taking their will back – like I did on certain occasions.'

Michael had been in contact with a correspondence course called 'Teen Challenge' for whom he had committed to work after his release. He implored his family to understand that money had never motivated his actions. After all, he'd grown up around money and it had never brought him happiness. 'I saw how it ruined me at times, and then

I saw what money on Wall Street did to me,' he proclaimed from behind bars.

Given time to think about his actions, he could now admit he'd often failed as a father to Lindsay. Prison life could be tough. Due to his celebrity status, Michael had been placed in protective custody. Many of the other inmates he shared a space with were the type of men who would probably wind up injured in a normal prison. Invariably, those 'types' included convicted paedophiles.

One day, Michael discovered several of them were keeping pictures of his daughter in their lockers. 'I had to really, really deal with patience, and control, and lots of things that I normally would never have to deal with in life,' he says, bowing his head with sadness. In spite of the emotional difficulties he faced on a daily basis, Michael still referred to prison as a 'blessing'. 'I think I really needed this dose of reality,' he said. Looking back over his life, Michael described himself as 'a control freak'. The only defence he could give for his actions was an overriding desire to protect his family. 'I wanted to control things; I wanted to control my life and other people's lives, my destiny… I didn't want people around my family, because I felt that they were a harm to them, or a threat to them.'

The words to Lindsay's song 'Confessions' had given Michael a lot to think about. They finally brought home the awful truth that he'd often failed her as a father. 'I think that they were touching, they were painful, and heart-warming, and very personal,' he said, his eyes glistening with tears. Pausing to compose himself, he continued, 'They really made me stop and think a lot, about everything in our life and even about myself. No matter what other people think, how they want to interpret it or view it, it made me feel loved.' Given time to take stock of his actions, Michael could finally begin reconstructing the shambles that currently constituted his life.

In contrast to his past suspicions about Lindsay's recreational activities, he now trusted her implicitly. 'She absolutely wouldn't do that,' he said, referring to her alleged use of drugs. As far as Michael was concerned, his beloved daughter hadn't put a foot wrong. 'I don't think anyone makes mistakes. I think we make decisions and we make choices. As far as I'm concerned, Lindsay hasn't made any mistakes in life, and it's all part of life.'

Despite his own stab at earning celebrity status, he was also ready to step away from the limelight. 'I leave that to the pros,' he laughed. 'I have no interest in showbusiness. It's shark-infested water out there and I give my daughter a lot of credit for withstanding all of the things they say.' All the signs suggested that Michael was finally beginning to confront his demons. His self-destructive and often maniacal tendencies had alienated everyone around him. It was hard not to pity Michael Lohan. But it was just as difficult to believe he really had turned over a new leaf. Only time would tell.

As for Lindsay, she was enjoying her newfound freedom as an adult. Like many teenagers keen to demonstrate their coming of age, she decided to get a tattoo. She opted for a tribute to her late grandfather, with the words '*la vita e bella*' (life is beautiful) tattooed on her lower back. 'I was on the phone with my grandmother when I got it because she's Italian and I wasn't sure. People were telling me all different ways to say it and I said, "Well, I don't [want to] have the wrong meaning on my back tattooed for life."' Already adept at handling so much emotional pain, Lindsay boasted that the tattoo was fairly painless. 'I was eating ice cream when I got this one. I was shocked that it didn't hurt,' she laughed.

Lindsay was also preparing to move into a new home. Her house-hunting endeavours had lasted almost an eternity, but finally she'd settled upon an apartment. Thankfully, her assistants could take care of all the paperwork. Her new pad was a three-bedroom condominium in the Sunset Strip area. Lindsay had paid a whopping $1.9 million, but she loved the place and it was worth every penny. Former *Friends* star Matthew Perry had a two-bedroom place in the same unit. The estate agents told Lindsay the complex had been built in the 1960s and, during that time, it had been home to a host of celebrity stars. Lindsay loved the idea that her new home had a history, and she couldn't wait to take her little sister up to the rooftop pool!

At one point, there was even talk of Lindsay returning to college. She had always been keen to study entertainment law, to give herself a better grip on the business. 'I could make sure my lawyers are doing what they say they're doing!' she giggled. 'I think it's really important to have an education.'

Her friends Mary-Kate and Ashley Olsen had already demonstrated that it was possible to combine an acting career with a college scholarship. 'I would go to NYU. I'm a New York girl, and it's easy to get to London and LA from here,' she mused. It was definitely something to think about.

But not everything in Lindsay's life was plain sailing. The paparazzi continued to monitor her every move and were quick to detect any remotely scandalous behaviour. The party-girl tag that Lindsay so detested would be round her neck for quite some time. When Lindsay missed an early-morning appearance on *Live with Regis and Kelly* after being spotted at the *King Kong* première the night before, people wondered whether the star had really turned over a new leaf. Pulling out at the eleventh hour, she left her helpless TV hosts in the lurch. 'Lindsay

Lohan is sick… she's not coming. Well, that's kind of a blow. She has food poisoning,' said a stunned Regis Philbin. Lindsay protested her innocence claiming she was genuinely ill. But, only hours later, she appeared on MTV having made a full recovery. She appeared on *Access Hollywood* to make a public apology. 'I know it came across really bad. I'll make it up to you, I swear!'

Further tales of hedonistic activity surfaced when it emerged that Lindsay had a new best friend – her fashion icon Kate Moss. Lindsay was thrilled to receive a dinner invitation to LA's Mr Chow from the disgraced supermodel. Both stars had a lot in common – they'd been hounded by the paparazzi, accused of drug-taking and had a secret passion for rock stars. They hit it off instantly.

There were rumours the new friends were planning a spa weekend together. Later, it was even alleged the pair had been spotted pole dancing (fully clothed) at strip club Scores, even kissing and caressing each other. Lindsay never substantiated the reports. But there was some truth to the rumour that Lindsay would be replacing Kate in a Chanel campaign at the request of Karl Lagerfeld. 'I'm so excited,' she squealed. 'I think it's for a magazine. I'm shooting with Karl Lagerfeld! It's amazing.' However, the world-famous fashion designer would later refute these claims in *New York* magazine, saying Lindsay

Lohan was too immature to handle such a large campaign. 'I prefer Nicole Kidman and that generation,' he disclosed.

For now, though, it seemed nothing could touch Lindsay Lohan. Any scandalous stories in the press only seemed to bolster her popularity even more. Once again, the ubiquitous starlet was in huge demand over the New Year period. She was booked to host a $200-a-ticket party at Miami club Privé and was even invited to do a DJ set! Lindsay had plenty of DJ friends and they'd shown her how to beat match in the past. For now, she'd probably just stick to fading the records in and out.

Lindsay also planned to use the trip as an excuse for a family holiday. She spent the day soaking up rays with her mum, while at night she breezed into the hottest restaurants and clubs. As a special thank you to Dina, Lindsay also splashed out on a makeover for her at Elizabeth Arden's Red Door Spa and Salon. 'My mom is a beautiful woman,' gushed Lindsay. 'She's amazing but she's working a lot and she's doing a lot of stuff for me and going through a lot with my family. She never takes any time for herself because there's four children to look after.'

Spending more time with her family was one of Lindsay's resolutions for 2006. She also intended to do more charity work. In the past, Lindsay had confessed a secret ambition to open up a chain of orphanages. 'There are kids around the world who have nothing. And I have so much. I want to be able to give back.'

Directly after the Hurricane Katrina disaster in New Orleans, Lindsay had taken a homeless girl under her wing. 'I was at dinner and there was this girl,' recalls Lindsay. 'She came to New York for the day and, ironically, she couldn't go back. So I kind of took her under my wing. I said, "Do you want to come and stay with us for the rest of the night?" It's just the scariest thought. I can't even imagine it.' But saving the world wasn't enough to keep Lindsay occupied. 'I'll think of more,' she said, attempting to list her goals for 2006. 'I give myself seven New Year's resolutions, because that's my lucky number.'

Any plans Lindsay might have for the following year, however, would be put on ice for the time being. After a riotous party in Miami, Lindsay Lohan opened her eyes to 2006 from a hospital bed.

18

FROM INNOCENCE
TO EXPERIENCE

From the age of two, Lindsay had suffered from bronchial asthma. All her life, she'd spent time in hospital as a result of attacks, and doctors even hinted that asthma might have been a contributory factor in her last two heavily publicised hospital stays.

Lindsay suffered another attack while in Miami to host New Year's celebrations and was rushed to the Mount Sinai Medical Center. An investigator from the TV show *Insider* reported that the attack had been so severe it had caused a broken blood vessel in her neck. 'I don't think people understand how truly terrifying it is to have an asthma attack,' her mother told the press. While not wishing to raise any alarm, she added, 'Lindsay has had bronchial asthma since she was two. She's completely fine.

Asthma... you can be fine in two days. She's a little girl, she'll be OK.'

Not everyone shared Dina's optimism. Lindsay's father expressed concern from his prison cell. 'Asthma has been a serious problem. She almost died from it when she was five, and one of her cousins died from it at 27.' But he went on to say, 'I'm very concerned for Lindsay. I'm hearing all these rumours about her partying too much.'

The supposed discovery of a pregnancy test kit in Lindsay's overnight bag made her hospital visit even more intriguing. It was alleged that a friend had smuggled the pregnancy test kit into Lindsay's ward, along with a bag full of goodies containing playing cards, mouthwash, Coke and a box of Cocoa Pops! Why Lindsay would need a home pregnancy test while she was in a hospital only indicated how ridiculous the stories surrounding her stay were becoming.

After three days, Lindsay was released from hospital. She admitted overworking and that going out too much had been the likely cause of her attack. 'I was tired,' she sighed. 'I was having a bunch of asthma attacks that led up to that and I was going through a time where I was overscheduling myself and not taking time for myself. Instead of resting, sometimes I wanted to go out and hang with my friends and go to a club which probably wasn't the best thing to do.'

Dina fiercely denied that her daughter had a drink or drug problem, but agreed that she needed to stop smoking. 'She smokes under a pack a day. She's addicted. The doctor put her on an anti-smoking pill. God willing, it will work within a month.'

Lindsay had also been warned by doctors to stay away from cats and dogs. Dina explained, 'Lindsay's on Advair [asthma medication]. She can't be around dogs and cats and certain foods. And, when you are 19, you don't deal with that. I am her mother and I tell her, "You have to stick to it."'

It wasn't an experience Lindsay would forget in a hurry. As a permanent reminder, she planned to have the word 'Breathe' tattooed on her wrist. She loved her last tattoo and couldn't wait to get another one. 'The attack was a big deal, so I wanted to commemorate it on my body,' she told friends.

One friend suggested it was a reminder to slow down and enjoy life. The tattoo also recalled John Lennon's famous quote: 'You are all geniuses, and you are all beautiful... You don't need anyone to tell you who you are... You are what you are... Get out there and get peace, think peace, live peace, and breathe peace, and you'll get it as soon as you like.'

Lindsay was due to start filming *Chapter 27*, the film about John Lennon's assassin Mark Chapman. Even before she embarked on the project, she'd been a huge fan of The Beatles. Her new role provided a great excuse to explore their work in greater depth.

Less than a week after Lindsay was released from hospital, however, she was seen out partying with her mother at New York club Bungalow 8. A witness reportedly saw Lindsay sipping from a champagne glass while sitting on 30-year-old Sean Lennon's lap. Dina, meanwhile, was in a separate booth with her new boyfriend. 'We had a late dinner and dropped by Bungalow to see a couple of friends,' sighed Dina. 'We were not drinking.'

Rumours that Lindsay might be dating John Lennon's famous son had been surfacing for some time. Although the pair had been acquainted for some time, Lindsay's role in *Chapter 27* had brought them closer. Keen to research her part properly, she called Sean and suggested they meet up. The pair were spotted enjoying dinner at New York restaurant Bette before heading off to meet Dina at a club. Dina remained coy about the liaison. 'Sean is a really good friend of hers. More power to them. I'm not going to say they're dating, or not dating.'

Comments made by Sean in music magazine *Q* suggested he was on the lookout for a girlfriend. He told journalists he was looking for any woman aged between 18 and 45 with an IQ above 130. 'They must not have any clinical, psychological disorders – and have a kind heart. I'm completely alone and I'm completely miserable,' he joked.

Lindsay clearly fitted the bill! The supposed relationship was obviously serious enough to annoy Sean's ex-girlfriend. Socialite Bijou Phillips was apparently overheard at LA club Teddy's screaming, 'Lindsay Lohan... dating Sean? How could he! How could he stand to be with her?'

In the space of just several weeks, Lindsay was romantically linked to several high-profile stars. One tabloid reported that the young star had been embroiled in a secret tryst with Leonardo DiCaprio! Apparently, he'd been a regular visitor at Lindsay's hospital bed, sneaking in through the back entrance wearing a cap to cover his face. Allegedly, he'd been showering Lindsay with chocolates and flowers and the couple were secretly planning a cruise in the Caribbean. But there appeared to be very little substance to the story.

The next minute, she was linked with *Jackass* and *Dukes of Hazzard* star Johnny Knoxville. The flirtatious teen was allegedly spotted with the married father at LA's Chateau Marmont. 'They were really close, walking together through the bungalows by the pool. They didn't seem to be acting too covertly, but that's because nobody was around.'

Lindsay rubbished such claims – she would never interfere with a married man. On a different occasion, she was supposedly spotted exchanging phone numbers with none other than Keanu

Reeves. Gossips claimed the pair struck up a conversation after meeting in the washrooms of a restaurant. They made eye contact in the lobby, chatted, complimented each other's work and finally asked the front desk for pen and paper to exchange numbers.

Then there was actor Nick Cannon. The pair had become friends on the set of *Bobby* and Nick had even presented his co-star with a VH1 Big In 05 'It' Girl award. When cornered by journalists at the event and asked whether romance might be blossoming, he replied, 'I'm very fond of her. She's a very beautiful person and a great friend of mine. And I probably wouldn't be here tonight if she weren't here.'

A more likely romantic candidate was her co-star in *Chapter 27*, 34-year-old Jared Leto. Speculation arose after Lindsay was spotted wearing a cryptic symbol on her foot, similar to one Jared uses when he signs autographs. Lindsay was also known to be a fan of Jared's band 30 Seconds to Mars, and had frequently been spotted in the audience. Adding more fuel to the fire, Lindsay had started sporting a silver 'J' on a chain around her neck. There were even some rumours the pair were planning to marry!

Lindsay refused to comment on a relationship with Jared, claiming, 'We're great friends.' In fact, Lindsay refused to be drawn into conversation about any potential love interests. 'There are people I like right now. There are people I have strong feelings for and who have a good impact on my life and I really respect them. They have the right outlook on things. I think that's really all I can ask for. Someone who genuinely cares about me and my happiness.'

But, for now, Lindsay wasn't looking for serious commitment. There would be plenty of time for that in the future. Taking full advantage of her age and position, she was determined to live out her young and carefree lifestyle while she still could. 'I like the chase,' she admitted. 'The second I know somebody likes me is the second I'll be like, "OK, bye." I'm young. It's not like I'm going to be engaged to anybody any time soon,' she smirked. 'Although it would be funny if I just randomly got married.'

She was reluctant to mention names, but Lindsay did confess to having crushes on several older men. 'I like the ones I probably shouldn't like... the rock star kind of people. I'm obsessed with Johnny Depp. Oh my God, because he's dark and cool and edgy and... dirty.' Ironically, Lindsay had wanted to test for a part in *Charlie and the Chocolate Factory*, but the producers had told her she was too old!

But she did resent being constantly linked to every granddad in the industry. 'People say I meet all these older men and sleep with them. That's disgusting. God knows where all those guys in this business have been! They should start picking on them a little more.' She maintained that she was still willing to date someone within the industry, but that the main quality she looked for in a man was honesty.

While Lindsay's love life was a constant source of speculation, even more dramatic revelations were yet to come with the publication of Lindsay's *Vanity Fair* interview. Famously, she'd agreed to pose naked for the shoot with world-famous photographer Mario Testino. Reticent at first, Paris Hilton's tasteful shots for the magazine finally convinced her. 'I haven't seen anything… I'm kind of scared,' she told journalists days before the publication came out.

The shoot had a '50s screen starlet theme based on Marilyn Monroe and Brigitte Bardot. As for the nudity, Lindsay explained, 'We just kind of went for it and decided to push the envelope. It was kind of my idea.'

Unfortunately, when the magazine did finally hit newsstands, Lindsay was left feeling devastated.

Admittedly, her pictures looked fantastic, but it was the details contained within the interview that upset her. Lindsay had confessed to interviewer Evgenia Peretz about her bulimic episodes and recounted her confrontation of the eating disorder backstage at *Saturday Night Live*. It was the first time any admission had been made in the press and confirmed rumours floating around for months previously.

A day later, the magazine alleged that Lindsay's

publicist Leslie Sloane Zelnik had attempted to remove any drug references from the interview.

Days after the interview broke, Lindsay's publicist refuted all allegations made in the magazine. However, *Vanity Fair* stood firmly by Peretz, describing her as a reputable journalist and pointing out that every word Lindsay had uttered was recorded as evidence on tape. *Star* magazine ran a follow-up article suggesting that several of Lindsay's friends were concerned for her health.

Of course, Lindsay was used to so-called friends telling tales to make money, so nothing really surprised her. However, her ex-boyfriend Wilmer did step forward to pledge his support if ever the suffering star should need it. 'I wish her the best and I hope she surrounds herself with the right people,' he said. 'If she ever needs me, I'll be there.'

When Lindsay suffered yet another hospital visit later that month, the press quickly seized on the story as an opportunity to suggest that the star was heading off the rails. In fact, it was only the press who seemed to be spiralling out of control; Lindsay had simply fallen and cut herself on a teacup.

The accident happened at singer/photographer Bryan Adam's $5 million mansion. Exasperated by so many lies, Dina explained, 'She and her friends were preparing breakfast, with eggs and everything, and Lindsay was going up the stairs, carrying a ceramic teacup. She had just come out of the shower so she was still wet and had some lotion on, and she completely flipped on the stairs since it was slippery. The teacup went flying, it was shattered, and one of the pieces cut Lindsay in her shin. It was an accident.' Dina went on to confirm that her daughter was in good health. 'She's totally fine. She's doing jumping jacks now!'

More scandal was in store, however, when Lindsay mislaid her personal journal while out partying with friends at Hiro in the Maritime Hotel. When she arrived home to find her precious book missing, the anxious star instantly burst into tears. She contacted everyone she'd been with that evening and demanded that the hotel staff conduct a thorough search of the building. But nothing turned up. Lindsay's diary contained deeply personal details about her life, secrets she probably wouldn't even share with Dina. Now some horrible tabloid journalist probably had his grubby hands on the book.

A columnist from the *New York Daily News* somehow came into possession of the diary, claiming entries from the last ten days contained juicy gossip about Jared Leto, someone believed to be Maroon 5 front man Adam Levine and Lindsay's family. He refused to divulge any further information – his scruples got the better of him. Although the diary was eventually returned to Lindsay, several pages had been torn out.

Almost immediately, Lindsay's lawyers issued a

legal document preventing any publication of material in the press. 'We appreciate the diary being returned, but unfortunately we are saddened by the fact that pages were stolen,' declared Lindsay's representatives.

Day and night, the Lindsay Lohan rumour mill never really stopped turning. The constant hum of Chinese whispers had become a backdrop against which Lindsay was accustomed to living. She'd been through so much in the last two years, so a few unsolicited tabloid scandals seemed like a blip on the horizon. Besides, Lindsay was older now. She knew her own limitations and had her priorities firmly in place. No one could take that learning experience away from her. 'My last year was kind of like my freshman year in college,' she reflected. 'I experienced going out all the time and hanging out with all these people, clubbing and just learning about it. But I kind of got over it really fast. But [the tabloids] continue to say I still go out. I just don't want people to think I'm in this business for the wrong reasons. I don't want them to be mistaken about the kind of person that I am.'

The past couple of years had definitely been tumultuous but, overall, Lindsay had no regrets. 'Growing through shit makes me that much stronger,' she claimed defiantly in the face of her critics.

Emerging from a dark and seemingly endless tunnel, Lindsay now had a much brighter outlook on life. 'Doing great things makes me want to do even better things,' she enthused. 'I want to do things that make me feel good, and work with charities and see the positive side of things. With the position I've kind of come into, I'm in a place where I can really make an impact on people and really help girls that are, you know, people with anorexia, people that aren't in good relationships with their lovers… people that don't get along with their parents. I can change that a little bit.'

Lindsay Lohan had changed; that much was clear. She was no longer the devout socialite, desperate to attend every party. 'I thought, if I didn't, I'd miss something,' she says of her past exploits. 'Totally screwed up my whole image.'

These days, she prefers to spend her time at home with friends, and even refers to herself as a 'homebody'. After doing it for so long, clubbing on a nightly basis has lost its glamorous appeal. 'Most of my friends are older and we aren't into always going out. We like to hang around the house and the beach and just relax,' she says. 'I pretty much don't leave the house! I just love to be in a place where there's a beach and water. I love listening to the sound of the ocean. What I want has changed. I have become much more practical. I'd rather go on a hike and go camping than go out to a club now. I still like to go out, but I'm growing as a person and I've found other ways to feel better.'

To prove her point, Lindsay draws attention to her 19th birthday celebrations. 'For my birthday, I flew to LA for the weekend and sat in a little restaurant and just, like, had dinner, went back to my friend's house and didn't do anything.' At the time, Lindsay had even joked she was holding a contest with a pal to see how many slices of birthday cake she could demand at different dinners.

Lindsay's new hair colour was also an indication of her willingness to stand out from the crowd. No longer the bottle blonde, she was now a dark and brooding brunette. The switch was for her new role in *Bobby*, but Lindsay professed to loving the new colour. 'I feel a bit classier with the darker hair... There's a lot of blondes out in LA, boys,' she laughed.

Prior to shooting the video for 'Confessions', Lindsay had taken a stroll along the beach to clear her head – something the old Lindsay would have been unable to comprehend. 'A year ago, I wouldn't have known to do that, to do something that was a bit more earthy to make yourself feel better, rather than going out and getting wasted.' Her basic needs were also a lot more modest. 'I used to want flashy cars. I still have this BMW 745 that's, like, white rims, blacked-out windows, so flashy. All I want to do is get rid of the car and get a jeep.'

By her own admission, Lindsay Lohan was growing up.

19

A FALL FROM GRACE

As Lindsay Lohan's teenage years drew to a close and she prepared to enter adulthood, looking back, she concluded that it had been a rough ride. Compared to her contemporaries, the sweet freckled-faced kid from Long Island had been forced to grow up quickly. But she had no regrets. Any mistakes she'd made were all part of life's learning curve. 'The past year has felt like five lifetimes because I've grown up a lot. I know better what to do and what not to do. I lost sight of the people and things that are most important to me.'

Now ready to move on with her life, Lindsay wanted to be taken seriously as both an actress and a person. Although she was grateful for the boost Disney had given her career, those saccharine days of childish movies were over. 'I hate it when people call me a teen queen,' she shuddered. 'I don't need to do any more kid movies. The word kid makes you feel like a child. Someone I dated called me a kid all the time. I hated it. I mean, everyone's a kid at heart but I feel like I've worked so hard and done so much all by myself.'

To the relief of those around her, she was also starting to take better care of her health. 'I'm into all natural vitamins every morning, along with flaxseed and iron pills.' She'd also begun to take cooking lessons in her spare time and even made a black and white angel cake for hotel staff at the Chateau Marmont, where she was in temporary residence.

'I've gained more confidence,' smiled Lindsay. 'Photo shoots have a lot to do with that. They've made me more comfortable with my body. I went through a phase where I didn't like my ankles, my legs. I wasn't treating my body the right way. Now I've learned how to.

'I like how I feel now. I'm healthy. I don't diet. I eat what I want to eat, and I eat when I'm hungry. I'm so active, and I'm stressed a lot when I'm working, so that keeps me thin. I'd like to get more toned. I want to get into a crazy workout phase.'

Lindsay's most recent film roles had required her to step up a gear and deal with adult issues, while, at the same time, real-life dramas were unfolding around her. While filming *Bobby*, one of Lindsay's best friends from school was admitted to hospital with meningitis. 'She was like a cousin,' said a trembling Lindsay. 'I was on the phone with her parents every single night, and just before she died I wanted to fly back to see her so badly. But I had an important scene coming up the next day so I had to stay and shoot it.'

Midway through the shoot Lindsay received the phone call she had been dreading. Her friend had passed away. Clasping her mouth in shock, Lindsay burst into tears. Fellow cast members gathered round to offer support. Putting on a brave face, she eventually returned to the set. Holding back the tears, she channelled all her emotions into the scene. 'That scene is really personal for me,' she recalls. 'It was the most tragic one I've ever had to do and required the most acting. Other roles I've had didn't require as much acting because my character was closer to my own age and experience. This time I had to go to that darker place and use that for my work.'

In a bid to break away from her wild-child image, Lindsay also revealed plans for a charity trip to Kenya. Usually she preferred to be discreet about her charity work – 'When I do charity I don't need the press there,' she once fumed – but on this occasion she chose to discuss her plans. She would fly out to work with the One Campaign organisation, set up to help AIDS sufferers and poverty victims.

'As with Brad Pitt and other celeb visits, it'll likely focus on where America is helping make a difference to save and change lives,' revealed spokesperson Meighan Stone.

Another area of Lindsay's career that appeared to be blossoming was her involvement in the fashion world. Even as a little girl Lindsay had been passionate about clothes. On her seventh birthday she was given a black dress with 'short and puffy' cap sleeves. 'It had little bows – but not too many... It was like Marc Jacobs. That's who I could see doing something like that.'

Lindsay insisted on wearing the dress almost every day. 'It sounds so materialistic, but I really wanted to wear it.' Whenever Dina and Michael argued, Lindsay would turn to the dress for comfort. It became her security blanket. 'It would land me on the worst-dressed-of-the-week list if I wore it today,' she chuckled. 'It was so bright and colourful. I just wanted to find the positive, and I found it through wearing that dress. I wore it every single day for almost a month straight, and I'd sneak it out of the closet and wear it to school, and my mom would say, "No, Lindsay, you can't wear this every day." I still have it.'

Over a decade later, Lindsay was still addicted to clothes. She joked to friends that shoes were her therapy. Whenever she felt low, she would slip on a pair of stilettos and suddenly she felt fantastic. 'If I'm having a bad day, I put on a pair of stilettos, some red lipstick and a great dress and I go shopping!'

Boutiques would even lock their doors to give Lindsay some privacy. 'I was in Chanel the other day. Love Karl Lagerfeld, all that jazz,' she declared, flicking her hair. 'So I walk in and it started to fill up with paparazzi and they were like, "Do you want us to lock the doors?" I was like, "Yeah, you probably should, because it's going to get crazy and I really want to shop right now." And so they lock the doors and I'm taking things off the mannequins because I'm like taking everything from the store... I think I should be a stylist.'

On another occasion, Lindsay was caught bowing down on the pavement in front of a store. 'The guy I was with thought I was crazy... but I appreciate fashion. I mean, I die for clothes.'

Lindsay's shopping trips became so extravagant that eventually she had no room in her wardrobe. 'I saved another room at the Chateau Marmont for a year that was just a closet!' she confessed. 'That's just normal. I talk about my impulses with my therapist – I have a shopping problem; I love to shop too much.'

Reports in the press suggested Lindsay was spending up to $1 million a year on clothes and that she was undergoing a course of hypnotherapy to cure her habit. 'Her closets are overflowing with things like $8,000 Prada dresses and $2,000 Balenciaga bags,' claimed her stylist Rachel Zoe. 'She has so many clothes; she never even wears some of them!'

But Lindsay was outraged by the claims. 'That is just a bunch of crap,' declared her publicist in response to the comments. 'There's no hypnotist. And Lindsay loves clothes, but the idea that she spent that much last year is completely stupid.'

But even Lindsay would admit that she now owned enough clothes to open a shop, which is exactly what she planned to do one day. 'If I ever do something with clothing, I would like to open a shop in Paris. And I'd only do it if Karl Lagerfeld was interested in having his clothes there. Or Tom Ford. Or Alexander McQueen. Or Jean Paul Gaultier or Proenza Schouler.'

Lindsay already had plenty of friends in the fashion world. She referred to Stella McCartney as 'a surrogate sister' and was in close contact with Donatella Versace. 'I met her through Andy LeCompte – he does my hair and also Madonna's. We hung out and totally clicked.'

Lindsay could also count Marc Jacobs and Chanel boss Karl Lagerfeld among her admirers. 'She is really funny and lively and greatly talented and beautiful,' cooed Marc Jacobs. 'I was in the Mercer hotel one night and Lindsay delivered pizza to my room. We text each other. She brings out the teenage instinct in me.'

Karl Lagerfeld felt equally protective of the young star. 'There is something very special and touching about her. One wants to protect her – perhaps against herself. She is so fragile and such a beautiful modern girl. She is a gifted actress and singer. You can single her out in a crowded place. She is so unique.'

Lindsay was very quickly becoming a style icon. Teenage girls would look to the actress for inspiration, while high-powered designers were keen to adopt her as their muse. Inundated with deliveries of clothes, there simply didn't seem to be enough days in the week to wear all her new outfits. When Lindsay received an invite to the 2006 Academy Awards, she leaped at the opportunity to show off her wardrobe and changed an impressive three times during the course of the evening.

'That night I had a little fashion moment with Madonna, who I think is completely genius,' she recalled. 'She was wearing Versace, too, and she goes to Guy [Ritchie], "Who's wearing better Versace?" And he didn't say anything. Mine was this elegant, long gown. Hers was elegant as well. It was beautiful, pink, and I'd never seen Madonna in a pale pink, and she looked gorgeous. It was just funny to have that moment. And then I ran to the bathroom to change because I promised my friend who works at Calvin Klein that I'd wear something from their line. I love them. They were all in there helping me change, including Winona Ryder. I was so embarrassed because I didn't want to come off like a complete floozy. And actually, before I changed for the *Vanity Fair* Oscar party, I wore this amazing Christian Lacroix dress, so I ended up wearing three dresses that night.'

While Lindsay didn't want people to think she was materialistic, she had to admit that clothes were an extremely important part of her life. 'I like the idea of being able to represent something that I really care about. And if young girls are going to look up to me and I love something like Chanel or Louis Vuitton, then they'll say, "Ooh! Lindsay really likes Chanel."'

Fashion magazines soon caught wind of Lindsay's obsession and invited the actress to take part in glossy magazine shoots. She loved every minute of it. 'I think fashion is such a beautiful thing, and photographers really appreciate beauty. I like being a part of that. Each time I hear the click of the camera, I get really excited. I'll think, Maybe I should be sad now, because I love seeing women cry in pictures. It gives off some sort of vulnerability, which everyone has, and it's relatable. Plus, in looking at the image, you can create any story you want.'

Not all photographers, however, were as kind to Lindsay. Paparazzi photographers continued to monitor her every move. By now she was a regular fixture in the gossip pages and details of her public life were often leaked to the public. She found the situation extremely frustrating and increasingly difficult to cope with. No other actress appeared to be hounded as much as Lindsay Lohan was. In interviews she compared herself to the tragic singer and actress Marilyn Monroe.

'I don't know what they have left to say,' she said, throwing her arms in the air. 'They've said everything. I don't know if it happens to everyone, but I sure know it happens to me. A little more than to anyone else... like Marilyn Monroe.

'I say Marilyn Monroe because if I were blonde that's who I'd want to be like. I use everything she's gone through when I'm upset. That's what I take from her. There's always tragedy in actors' lives. People like drama. They feed off that.'

And there was certainly plenty of drama in Lindsay's life – namely among her high-profile circle of friends. In May 2006, Lindsay was reportedly involved in a public slanging match with the socialite Paris Hilton. The former friends stunned fellow clubbers at the trendy Hollywood spot Hyde. Paris's representative Elliot Mintz explained, 'Paris was having a conversation with a couple of friends. Lindsay approached her table and at that moment Paris felt she was being interrupted and didn't wish to speak to Lindsay. A couple of words were exchanged and Lindsay went back to her table. I can understand how other patrons in the club could have thought it had been a bigger deal than it actually was.'

But gossip website Tmz.com claimed there was a further source of tension. Paris was allegedly annoyed with Lindsay for mentioning her name in interviews with the media to help further her own career. The pair were also embroiled in an argument over Paris's on/off boyfriend Stavros Niarchos III, as Lindsay was allegedly making moves on the Greek shipping heir. The heiress confronted her nemesis at the trendy New York club Butters. 'She went off on this Stavros thing,' revealed Lindsay, 'grabbing my arm, saying, "I can't believe you f**king called Stavros."'

The situation escalated when Paris Hilton's former lover Brandon Davis launched a scathing attack on the actress. In a videotape leaked to the press, the 'Who's Your Daddy' star attacked Lindsay's personal hygiene, her lifestyle and lovers. 'I think she's worth about seven million. Which means she's really poor. It's disgusting, she lives in a motel.' He then went on to racially insult Lindsay's ex-boyfriend Wilmer Valderrama, saying, 'Is he in a mariachi band?' Paris could be seen giggling in the background.

Lindsay was furious and demanded Brandon make a public apology and donate $250,000 to charity. The situation grew worse when oil heiress Barbara Davis

(Brandon's grandmother) claimed Lindsay was in fact dating her grandson! Lindsay's publicists released a statement: 'It is unfortunate that Barbara Davis is desperate enough to make up a lie about Lindsay dating her grandson. Lindsay took the high road and accepted Brandon's apology last week, but they are not dating and they did not go to dinner together.'

But no sooner had Lindsay put the feud with Paris behind her than new reports emerged suggesting she had fallen out with Jessica Simpson. Lindsay allegedly lost her temper when the pop star refused to thank her for sending a tray of drinks over to her table at a Hollywood bash. Lindsay refuted the story, claiming she was actually one of Jessica's biggest supporters. 'I did not go into this industry to be shown on the cover of some magazine fighting with Jessica Simpson, who I think is a sweet girl. She's going through a divorce, and it's hard enough for her. They [tabloids] basically said I was verbally harassing this girl. I'm not that person.'

The last thing Lindsay wanted was to be portrayed as a victim, but it did seem as if everyone was out to get her. In July, she received a further blow when hackers broke into her Blackberry and sent offensive messages to friends. Lindsay's publicist revealed the perpetrator had sent had sent 'disgusting and very mean messages that everyone thought were coming from Lindsay. They weren't. We now have lawyers looking into it. Some people think Paris may have been involved because the wording of the messages sounds very familiar.'

Paris Hilton was rumoured to be involved with the scandal, but vehemently denied she had anything to do with it. Her representative Elliot Mintz reported, 'I'm saddened this happened to Lindsay. I lived through this with Paris two years ago when her Sidekick was hacked into, and the loss of privacy is unbearable. But, as for any suggestion that Paris would have anything to do with this, that is silly, untrue and unfortunate.'

But the phone hacking continued. Lindsay was convinced Paris and ex Brandon were the culprits. 'I started getting prank calls from them on my voicemail. They'd be screaming and saying stuff that was said in the video,' she fumed.

Paris found herself in hot water when it emerged she had an account with internet site SpoofCard.com. The virtual calling card allowed users to dial a toll-free number, then key in the destination number and the Caller ID number to display. The service also provided optional voice scrambling to make the caller sound like someone of the opposite sex.

Once it became apparent customers were abusing the service, SpoofCard.com were forced to act quickly. They confirmed 50 accounts had been terminated, including one belonging to Paris Hilton. They also revealed that Lindsay was among those whose voicemail accounts had been hacked. 'Paris was entering unauthorised mail boxes,' announced SpoofCard attorney Mark Del Bianco. 'A number of the 50 persons were making unauthorised entrances to Miss Lohan's voicemail.'

Lindsay's publicist declared, 'I have turned this matter over to Lindsay's lawyers.'

The whole episode was extremely humiliating. No matter how hard she tried, it was impossible to maintain any privacy. Even former friends and lovers seemed happy to air her dirty laundry in public. Wilmer Valderrama shocked listeners of the Howard Stern radio show when he revealed intimate details of his sex life, naming Lindsay as one of the best women he'd ever slept with. He also revealed that he had videotaped his sexual escapades on numerous occasions, but erased the tapes to keep them from being leaked on the internet. Fortunately, Lindsay saw the funny side and was even flattered by his remarks. 'It's good to be friends with exes because, at one time, they made you happy. I'm more positive now. I used to be negative and be like "You ruined my life!"'

In the past Lindsay had been linked to a string of eligible males. She insisted she was single, but claimed there were several potential candidates on the scene. 'It sounds cheesy, but I have people who are fun to have crushes on. Sleeping around is not something that interests me, but the act of love is an amazing thing. It's groovy. You've gotta have some fun and let those emotions out.'

On 2 July 2006, Lindsay celebrated her 20th birthday. True to form she planned to celebrate in spectacular style. After much deliberation she settled on a 'Great Gatsby'-themed party on Malibu beach. And, if that wasn't enough, Disneyland California also stepped in to throw a party for the young star. Officials invited Lindsay and her friends to spend an evening in both Anaheim parks. Limousines arrived at the Great Californian Hotel shortly after 10pm on a Friday night.

Once day visitors had cleared the park, Lindsay and her pals were given free rein on the rides. At 1.30am the party boarded the Sailing Ship Columbia with Mickey Mouse and cruised around the rivers of America. Waiters dressed in pirate outfits served plates of food and drinks. Lindsay was even presented with a birthday cake of her own face.

Several days later, however, reports emerged suggesting Lindsay and her friends had upset Disney staff by engaging in raucous behaviour. One blogger on Miceage.com, a website dedicated to the Anaheim theme park, claimed, 'Between the rude behavior and the snotty attitude the entire party displayed, there were very few Lindsay Lohan fans working at Disneyland by the end of that night.'

Lindsay refuted the accusations with a statement from her publicist: 'Lindsay was very happy that Disney let her have her birthday there. She had the best time. The rest of the story was complete bull.'

Fortunately, Lindsay's other birthday party proved much less controversial. During her birthday bash in Malibu, Lindsay's lawyer friend Mike Heller introduced her to restaurateur Harry Morton. Harry came from a wealthy stock: his father Peter was co-founder of Hard Rock Café, while his uncle Arnold was founder of the Morton's Steakhouse Chain, and Harry himself was President and CEO of the Pink Taco restaurants.

The couple clicked and spent the evening deep in heavy conversation. From that moment on, they were inseparable. The couple were spotted in partying together at the Hyde Lounge and sharing dinner at the Chateau Marmont, and they spent the Fourth of July holiday week in Malibu lounging at Harry's plush apartment, blasting Led Zeppelin through the stereo.

Inevitably, the couple were followed everywhere, and, when the media attention became unbearable, Harry suggested they should take a holiday in Hawaii. Shortly afterwards, Harry accompanied Lindsay to the Venice Film Festival, for the premiere of her movie *Bobby*, and the pair were photographed taking a romantic boat trip around the city's famous canals. Lindsay even sparked rumours of an engagement by wearing a sparkler on the red carpet.

Earlier that month Harry had been spotted buying a ring at Cartier in Beverly Hills. A spokesperson for the restaurateur reported, 'I can confirm that Harry was shopping in Cartier, but what he purchased I cannot confirm. If it was in fact a gift, then that's between him and whomever the gift is for.'

However, Lindsay's mum later told journalists, 'They're not engaged.' According to friends, Lindsay was merely teasing the press. The bauble Harry bought for Lindsay was a trinity ring. 'It's not an engagement ring but a very sweet gift. Harry's an angel,' said Dina. 'He's a great guy and he's been a great influence on her... They love each other and care for each other. They're dating and it's moving along.'

Harry was also supportive of Lindsay in her times of need. Friends hoped he would help the actress settle down, putting an end to her wild-child image and providing some much needed stability in her life. Lindsay felt extremely lucky to have Harry by her side; the last couple of years had been difficult and she was tired of coping alone. But it wouldn't be that easy to leave behind the party lifestyle. In spite of Harry's advice, she continued to party hard and burn the candle at both ends. 'Clubbing is my life!' she exclaimed to one magazine.

However, it would also be her downfall. Lindsay's nightlife antics would inevitably take their toll on both her career and personal relationships.

20

FACING THE MUSIC

By now Lindsay Lohan's career was on a roll. Having demonstrated she could handle difficult roles, she had successfully made the transition from teen star to adult actress. Her next major project was *Georgia Rule*, the story of a rebellious teenager who is hauled off by her alcoholic mother to spend the summer in a Mormon town with her grandmother. Over the course of the summer, family secrets are uncovered and the three women become closer than ever before. Lindsay was cast in the role of Rachel, alongside Jane Fonda and Felicity Huffman. 'My character's overtly sexual,' said Lindsay with a wink. 'It's something I haven't really done before. She's a complete Lolita.'

It was a powerful role. Unfortunately for Lindsay,

the drama would continue even once the cameras had stopped rolling. While filming scenes in Los Angeles, the fragile actress was rushed to hospital after collapsing from heatstroke and exhaustion. According to a representative, 'She was overheated and dehydrated... She was filming in 105-degree Fahrenheit weather for 12 hours.'

Doctors gave Lindsay a Vitamin B shot and kept her under observation for two hours.

However, it later transpired that Lindsay had been out clubbing the night before at Hollywood haunt Guy's. 'She was definitely partying. She wasn't over the top, but having a great time.'

Lindsay herself claimed to be out for a friend's birthday. 'I tried to please my friend and I ended up getting sick,' she told a magazine. 'It's about learning to say no more than yes. I'm a people-pleaser. But you can't always make everyone happy.'

But Lindsay's hospital trip was not really surprising. She already had a reputation for turning up late on set and delaying filming, and, aside from a few rumblings, Lindsay was usually given the benefit of doubt. But on this occasion she had gone one step too far.

James G Robinson, the CEO of Morgan Creek Productions – who were bankrolling *Georgia Rule* – decided to intervene. He sent a scathing letter to the actress calling her 'discourteous, irresponsible and unprofessional'. He compared her actions to those of a spoiled child and claimed she had 'endangered the quality of this picture'. He went on to say, 'We are well aware that your ongoing heavy partying is the real reason for your so-called "exhaustion".' He also threatened to sue Lindsay if she continued to delay production.

Lindsay was humiliated when the letter was leaked on the internet. Dina quickly jumped to her daughter's defence, saying the letter was 'too much' and that Lindsay was 'a wonderful child'. But the floodgates had now been opened and disgruntled crew members took the opportunity to back up Robinson's accusations. One crew member on *Herbie: Fully Loaded* branded Lindsay 'irresponsible and unprofessional'. Another anonymous source told the gossip website PageSix.com, 'Her behavior [on *Georgia Rule*] is exactly the same inconsiderate s**t she pulled on the *Herbie* production. She stayed out all night, and then the doctor announced that Ms Lohan had asthma the next day. She played the exhaustion card a couple of times. She called in sick one day and she is across town [spending] a day with her then-boyfriend Wilmer Valderrama.'

The veteran actor William H Macy also blasted Lindsay for her conduct during the filming of *Bobby*, insisting she 'should have her a** kicked'. Although he admired her talent, he did not like her manners.

'You can't show up late. It's very, very disrespectful… I think what an actor has to realise [is that], when you show up an hour late, 150 people have been scrambling to cover for you. It's nothing but disrespect. And Lindsay Lohan is not the only one. A lot of actors show up late as if they're God's gift to the film. It's inexcusable, and they should have their a**es kicked.'

US chat show host Rosie O'Donnell also publicly weighed in with her opinion. 'Lindsay's behaviour was unacceptable. It's not like she was doing *Dumb & Dumber 2*. It's a Jane Fonda movie! Be early! I saw [Lohan] stumbling around a club drunk [once] and her mother was going, "She's all right!" I can say this from experience: it's hard to be famous, and she's not doing it well at this point. But she'll get into rehab, take care of the eating disorder, and be all better in two years and have a huge comeback.'

Lindsay's co-star Jane Fonda hoped the young actress had learned her lesson. It was time Lindsay cleaned up her act and fully realised her acting potential. 'I think every once in a while a very, very young person who is burning both ends of the candle needs to have somebody say, "You know you're going to pay the piper – you better slow down." So I think it was good. She's in the magazines, so you always know what she's doing because you can just read about it in the tabloids. She parties all the time…

She's young and she can get away with it. But it's hard after a while to party very hard and work very hard. I want to say to her, "This is not a dress rehearsal. This is it. If you blow it, you don't get a second chance."'

During filming, Jane and Lindsay had formed a close bond of friendship. The pair even purchased matching orange Hermes bangles. The 68-year old veteran felt extremely protective towards the vulnerable star. 'I just want to take her in my arms and hold her until she becomes grown up. She's so young and she's so alone out there in the world in terms of structure and, you know, people to nurture her. And she's so talented. Oh my gosh, she can access emotion like nothing. And she just makes me cry. She made me cry a lot and when she was on the set she was really good; it's going to be a good movie.'

Lindsay took the friendly criticism on board. 'She was just trying to help,' she shrugged. 'They always try to do that with younger actresses. Jane's amazing. She's still hot. And sexy.'

But Lindsay didn't learn her lesson. Refusing to keep a low profile, she kept up her social engagements and was photographed emerging from several different nightspots. But it wasn't only clubs Lindsay failed to keep away from. In September, she was admitted to hospital again – this time with a fractured wrist. Lindsay had slipped over during a

New York Fashion Week party at Milk Studios. She was wearing flat boots at the time and couldn't understand what had happened. Her publicist suggested an investigation would be launched to determine whether Milk Studios had taken adequate health and safety precautions with the ground.

After a few hours in casualty, it emerged Lindsay had broken her wrist in two places, and doctors told her she would need to wear a cast for six weeks. It was another blow for Lindsay, and the studio bosses on *Georgia Rule* would not be happy.

Harry Morton leaped to his girlfriend's side to offer her moral support. He also suggested she should make an appointment with his cousin, who happened to be a specialist. Fortunately, Lindsay was able to remove the cast so her filming wasn't completely interrupted. 'She won't be doing cartwheels,' Dina told the press. 'But the cast is removable, so she can take it off for a short time, or she can wear long sleeves.'

Lindsay realised she would have to pay some serious attention to her career, and family and friends gathered round to offer support. Initially, Harry was a pillar of strength to the actress, leaping to his girlfriend's side to offer her moral support. He also suggested she should make an appointment with his cousin, who happened to be a specialist. But Harry was beginning to have trouble coping with her party lifestyle and fast living. And, as pressures mounted, cracks started to appear in the relationship.

Lindsay was spotted looking distraught on the patio of Chateau Marmont. Clasping her cell phone tightly, she was weeping on to a friend's shoulder. According to reports later published in the tabloids, Harry had dumped Lindsay, citing her partying as the cause. 'She was too much drama,' said a source close to Harry. 'Lindsay did cut down on the partying, but with her it's all relative. Harry is sober. It wasn't the partying that broke them up. Harry's more low-key and not into the same stuff she's into.'

Lindsay denied the rumours. But, just days later, Harry's publicist confirmed that the couple were 'taking a break'. Harry appeared on US show *Extra* saying, 'We're just sort of taking a little breather right now and slowing things down.' He admitted he had difficulty dealing with a high-profile relationship. 'A lot of people started saying we're engaged and it put a lot of pressure on things. We need a little space... I'm a very private person. I'm sure she [Lohan] has dealt with it [publicity] for years but it puts a lot of pressure on me... I have nothing but the utmost respect for Lindsay.'

Lindsay was distraught. She would later blame ructions in her private life for her lack of professional conduct on the set of *Georgia Rule*. 'It upset me because I was a bit irresponsible. I didn't think about the consequences but I was also going through something in my life.'

Once the tabloids caught wind of her split from Harry, Lindsay was linked to a number of eligible males. Even if she just spoke to a man, it was automatically assumed he must be her boyfriend. Rather than get irritated by the press, Lindsay chose to play games with journalists. 'I say things that aren't true a lot,' she told one magazine. 'If I was dating one person I'd probably tell them I was dating someone else and then I'd call my friend and be like, "Do you mind if I say that we're dating?" I figure I'll fuck with them [tabloids], because they fuck with me.'

These days Lindsay didn't might being linked to a string of celebrities and actors. 'In the past it would suck because they would just name every older man,' she sighed. 'I mean, I would be dead if I slept with that many people. But I know it's going to happen. But certain people...' she paused to grin. 'Certain people are true.'

Although ultimately Lindsay wanted a relationship, right now she wasn't ready to settle down with one person. While she was young, it made sense to play the field and sample the different options on offer. 'If I'm going to give my body to someone, I'd rather them not be with other people, but I want to be able to date if I like someone else. I don't think I've had enough experience with dating one guy for a long time.'

But after a while Lindsay wondered if she could ever settle down. 'I don't know if I could be monogamous,' she pondered. 'I don't want to be with just one person. I like being able to be in different relationships – being able to see a few people. And I'm not into cheating. It's better not to be in a relationship. I'm having fun right now.

'It is the variety of partners everyone likes, especially at my age. I'm like Angelina Jolie, taking on lovers. I don't need a steady relationship... I mean, if the sex is bad, the relationship's not going anywhere. Anyway, I don't even think I have had my best kiss yet.'

Lindsay credited the sitcom *Sex And The City* for inspiring her laidback dating philosophy. '*Sex And The City* changed everything for me, because those girls would just sleep with so many people.' However, she confessed most men found her new approach intimidating. 'I've heard that guys are intimidated by me even though I'm not an intimidating person. I'm honest and straightforward and people aren't used to that. I've become the guy in relationships.'

Besides, for the time being, Lindsay had to put her work first. She had too much going on in her life to consider another person. 'I need to focus on my career and getting my life in order. I don't want any distractions so I'm not ready to settle down with anyone yet. I feel blessed just to be where I am right now... But there is a boy I like in London.'

Although Lindsay never made a public declaration, it was obvious the 'boy' in question was Calum Best. The son of the late football legend George Best, notorious for his own wild ways, Calum had a reputation as a serial womaniser. The pair met in November 2006 when Lindsay was in London for promotional work. They allegedly made eye contact at Soho club Kabaret's Prophecy and eventually left together.

They spent every night together and were sighted at various trendy hotspots including the club Boujis. While on one wild night out, Lindsay narrowly escaped injury when her Range Rover collided with a police car. The newspapers had a field day, but Lindsay was far too preoccupied with her passenger.

It was obvious the couple fancied each other. But Lindsay had work commitments and was forced to return home. But the couple stayed in touch and six months later they embarked on a relationship. 'She invited me to New York for a premiere, so I went along,' Calum told *OK* magazine. 'After that, we headed to Paradise Island in the Bahamas to chill out away from it all and it's going well. It's early days but it's going real great. She's a fantastic girl, so watch this space, I guess.'

Some were dubious as to whether Calum could

remain faithful to Lindsay. There were even reports Lindsay had demanded hotel security prevent him from leaving the premises after she feared he might be checking out to visit another woman. But Calum insisted he was a changed man. 'I've been young, free and single and sowing my oats since I was 15 years old, but I've now reached a point where, if I had a girlfriend, I could commit to her and put in 110 per cent.'

Lindsay loved the fact that Calum was from London. She fell in love with the city when she'd visited with her then boyfriend Harry Morton in 2006. 'I just love Notting Hill – it has some really cool shops and great restaurants,' she said at the time. 'I've been looking at some properties while I've been over here and we're hoping to buy something soon. I can see me and Harry really fitting in there.'

Although Lindsay was happy, associating with party animal Calum did little for her reputation. Fed up with the constant criticisms of her lifestyle, she hit back at the tabloids. 'I go out because it's a release,' she fumed. 'Going out for me is about seeing my friends and not working. Being seen is just something that comes along with it. People think, Oh, she just wants to go out to all these places. That's what you read in the tabloids. But it has nothing to do with why I'm in this industry. Sure, you can cut the line at the clubs, but, at the end of the day, cutting the line at Bungalow 8 is not what's going to make me feel good.'

Lindsay felt extremely comfortable in clubs. Going out was more than a hobby – it had become a way of life. 'You know, a friend of mine just asked me, "What is it about the night time that you like?" First of all it's the only time that I have off. And I'm a night owl to begin with – I have complete insomnia. But the night is so much more serene to me. It's the only time I have to think, to just sit in my room and write and collect all my thoughts from the day. Maybe that's why I'm so into vampires, the night owl of it all.

'I'm 19 years old. I never went to college, and I never got to go through that phase. I'm not saying that if I were in college I would have gone through a crazy stage of going to frat parties and sorority houses and that sort of thing. But I think that people like to enjoy themselves. They do that stuff because they want to feel normal; they want to be out with other people. I'm like that. Also, sometimes I do things as research for a film.'

Lindsay also believed that part of the reason she was picked on by the press was because of her honesty. 'No one is perfect. It's not interesting to be perfect. You have to do stupid things. You have to do crazy things sometimes, whether you're in the public eye or not. At this point I could have done so many things, and I might as well have, because they're going to write I did them anyway. But you have to learn and go through things and experience life.'

In theory, the fun-loving young woman appeared to be on top of things, but the reality was very different. No matter how great an actress she was on screen, it was impossible to maintain the real-life pretence any longer. In December 2006, Lindsay admitted she'd been attending Alcoholics Anonymous meetings for a year. 'I've been going to AA for a year by the way,' she revealed nonchalantly. Why had she never mentioned this before? 'Well, it's no one's business. That's why it's anonymous!'

Despite her admission, Lindsay insisted she didn't have a problem. 'I didn't feel bad before. I never felt bad. I just wanted to, like, find a balance. I was out too much. I was too caught up. I mean, I'm 20 years old. I was off from work, I was getting ready to start a film, and I was like going out just to get it out of my system. I was going out too much and I knew that, and I have more to live for than that. But I don't drink when I go to clubs. I drink with my friends at home, but there's no need to. I feel better not drinking. It's more fun. I have Red Bull.

'I've lived with the impact of addictions my whole life with my father, and it takes a toll on everyone. And I don't want that. I don't necessarily know that I'm an addict. I only know that it's very hard to live your life as a double life. To make myself happy as well as everyone else. Because that's just in me: to keep everyone around me happy.'

Her main aim was to shift the focus from her party lifestyle to her career. The press coverage of her social life had got way out of hand. 'I was like, I don't want to be written about at these clubs with these people. I work, I act, I have a living. That's what I do every day. I work every single day.'

Dina was extremely proud and supportive of her daughter. Speaking to *American Idol* host Ryan Seacrest's KIIS-FM radio show, she stressed Lindsay was not an addict. 'You know, a lot of people she hangs out with go, and it's a positive thing. As a parent, you tell them what you can tell them, but she's 20 and I'm not gonna say, "Stay home and don't go out," that's a ridiculous thing to do. I'm there for support, and I'll obviously give her my opinion, but she's very smart.'

For a while, it seemed Lindsay had curbed her wild-child ways, but with temptation at every turn she found it impossible to give up clubbing completely. In January 2007, she was rushed to hospital for emergency surgery to remove her appendix. But just days later she was seen out partying in Miami.

However, the final straw came on 16 January when Lindsay allegedly passed out at Prince's post-Golden Globes party. Headlines were splashed across the tabloids the following morning. Lindsay was devastated. 'I never passed out in my life. I never vomited from having drinks. Like in public. I would never do that. Well… A few times. Well, everyone does in high school. It's living. Learning from your mistakes.'

Whether the stories were accurate or not, Lindsay accepted it was time to take action. Like countless celebrities before her, she decided to enter rehab. She released a public statement to the press: 'I have made a proactive decision to take care of my personal health.'

Lindsay arrived at the Wonderland Centre in LA holding a Jamba Juice smoothie in one hand and a Balenciaga bag in the other. 'You have to hit rock bottom sometimes to get yourself back to the top,' she later confessed. 'I always said I would die before I went to rehab, but I guess things change. Everyone's tired of hearing things about me and I think it's better I just lie low and get better.'

Lindsay remained vague about the real reasons why she entered rehab. 'It was just a lot of stuff,' she said hesitantly. 'Ultimately people that are around me know that if I want to do something then I'm going to do it, and you can't stand in my way. I'm a tough cookie. And I'm Irish-Italian so I've got a really bad temper! A lot of it for me was clearing my head, because I'm not really a crazy addict. Well, I enjoy having sex!'

Dina praised her daughter's decision to enter rehab. 'I'm so proud of her. She's really in a good place right now, spiritually and mentally. She's in an amazing, phenomenal place. She's 20 and she's solid, and she's doing what she needs to do. I don't know that many people who are that secure. It's all about her, and getting back on track. She's fine – she's amazingly fine.'

Dina denied that poor parenting was to blame for Lindsay's situation. 'She's from an addictive personality genetically,' she protested. 'And, in that world, they give you things like candy. "Hurt your ankle? Let's give her something." Lindsay had to fall and get up. I knew it was coming. I told her, but finally she was like, "Mommy, I had to do it myself." You can lead a horse to water. You can't make him drink.'

Entering the centre involved several sacrifices. Lindsay was unable to attend the screening of her film *Chapter 27* at the Sundance Film Festival. She checked into the centre for a 30-day period but was allowed to leave during the day to film her new movie *I Know Who Killed Me*. 'She will continue working but will spend her nights at the recovery facility,' revealed her publicist.

Initially, Lindsay found it difficult to adjust to her new lifestyle. 'I can't just sit still somewhere all day,' she complained. 'I was working so I'd be like "OK wait, I don't understand how I can be going to work but I can't go take a drive because I need to clear my head…" 'cause they expect you to go and get loaded or something. I guess they have to treat everyone as if it's the worst thing possible. It's standard.'

But staff at the Wonderland Centre found it equally difficult to deal with Lindsay. Although they dealt with celebrities on a daily basis, they had never encountered so much harassment from the press. 'They've had other celebrities there, just not as hardcore as me,' concluded Lindsay. 'Like paparazzi sitting outside of the house and taking pictures from far away. Or helicopters. The people didn't get why, when we would go to meetings, instead of being in the back of the car I would be like "I think I should drive, because they're going to chase you and it's going to be scary and we might get in an accident, and we don't need that." ' Lindsay admitted she liked to be in the driving seat: 'Because I can be calm.' Plus, she mischievously added, 'Because once in a while it's fun.'

When Lindsay eventually emerged from the centre 30 days later, she was extremely proud of her achievement. She claimed to have replaced alcohol with a new addiction – Kombucha, a detoxifying tea brewed from yeast and bacteria. 'I'm great, I feel wonderful,' she beamed. 'My motto is: Live every day to its fullest – in moderation!'

Lindsay would still attend the centre as an outpatient. 'She will continue as an outpatient. She will take it day by day. She's in it for the long haul, and she asks that her privacy be respected,' said her publicist.

She also admitted the sharp wake-up call was exactly what she needed to turn her life around. 'I was really sick. I went to hospital and had people sit me down who said, "You are going to die if you don't take care of yourself." I heeded what they were telling me.' Now she was ready to start again. She even bought two puppies to complement her new homebody lifestyle. 'Sober impulse buying of companions who will help me stay home,' she smiled.

These days Lindsay could laugh at newspaper stories. While relaxing with her pal DJ Samantha Ronson, she found an online blog about the alleged alcoholism. 'Lindsay Lohan has been out partying and drinking every night since she arrived in New York,' read Samantha out loud. 'So, rehab didn't work for her at all. What the hell was she doing in there? While everyone else was getting treated for addictions she was probably playing Hungry Hungry Hippos, clapping her hands excitedly, going "Look at the hippos eat! They're so hungry!"'

'I did checkers!' exclaimed Lindsay, laughing.

Most importantly of all, rehab had given Lindsay some much needed focus on her career. 'I noticed how much better I was – how much more clear my thoughts were. There are no distractions. Acting comes more naturally. It's not so much a job… Everything that I go through I use when I'm working. It just kind of happens. There's a way of dealing with hardships that are healthier than going out. That's what I've learned.'

Now her health was back on track, Lindsay was eager to demonstrate her capabilities as a serious actress. She hoped her performance in *I Know Who Killed Me* would do that very job. 'I don't think there has been a role for an actress like this movie was for me in so long. At first I was like, "I can't do this, I'm getting my legs cut off. I don't want to look like that in scenes, I want to look decent." But that was just me being young and stupid. And I have my first sex scene in it, which I always said I wouldn't do.

'I wanted to do this movie so people can see that I'm a fucking actress and I've been doing it forever and it's about time people see that. It felt so good to really act. I just pray people won't rip me apart for it, and be negative. The thing with the press, and why they need to leave me the fuck alone for a little bit, is because I don't want that distracting from my work. I want to get a nomination. I want to win an Oscar. I want to be known for more than going out. For being the "party girl". I hate that. I bust my ass when I'm filming and, when I have time off, yeah, I like to go out and dance.'

As part of her preparation for the film, Lindsay took up pole-dancing classes. She took lessons from Shiela Kelly who developed 'S Factor: Aerobic Striptease Workout and Pole Dancing'. Much to Lindsay's embarrassment, however, an email concerning her exploits was leaked to the press. 'They're all whores, they're all whores… except for some obviously!' read the subject line. She went on to say, 'So… 3 hours of pole dancing and bruised. Everywhere… I mean we're talkin' like, UPPER AND INNER THIGH ACTION-bruised… like a walking black-and-blue mark. I mean really though, really, I didn't know it was actually possible to have bruises in such areas of the body. Strippers dude, I tell you, I really respect the c***s now… I'm not gonna lie to ya.'

Lindsay issued an immediate apology through her publicist. 'Her character is a stripper, and she now realises that the job isn't easy. We should give these women credit,' said Leslie Sloane Zelnik.

But the embarrassments didn't end there. In May 2007, a series of images appeared in the *News of the World*, allegedly depicting Lindsay snorting cocaine with friends in an LA club. An unnamed pal revealed, 'She is inconsolable. She's convinced that everyone is out to get her.'

Her lawyer Mike Heller refused to confirm whether the shots showed Lindsay using drugs, but said, 'This just goes to show how hard it is to be Lindsay Lohan, who's even denied her privacy in the sacred confines of a ladies'-room stall and then must fend off the slings and arrows of false allegation.'

In a further blow, photos of Lindsay and the actress Vanessa Minnillo playing with knifes also appeared on the internet. Both girls were shown cavorting with knifes and pulling at each others' top.

And worse was to come. On 28 May 2007, Lindsay was arrested on suspicion of driving under the influence. At around 5.30am on a Saturday night, she lost control of her Mercedes convertible, hitting a kerb and trees. She was taken to Century City Hospital where she was treated for minor injuries. Police found a small amount of cocaine at the scene of the crash.

Earlier that evening, Lindsay was spotted at the West Hollywood nightclub Les Deux. She was seen leaving the venue at 3.30am, an hour and a half after closing time. California's Department of Alcoholic Beverage Control (ABC) set up an investigation to ascertain whether underage youths were served alcohol on the premises.

The club issued a statement: 'We have and will continue to work closely with the ABC to make sure alcohol is consumed by responsible people of the legal drinking age, in a responsible manner. Les Deux is a restaurant and there is no age limit for our patrons. Lindsay had dinner at Les Deux that night and waited for friends to pack up the DJ supplies, thus leaving Les Deux after closing. Because of the enormous paparazzi presence outside of Les Deux that night, we allowed her to stay late and wait for her friends. She was not drinking at Les Deux, and left driven by her driver.'

After hearing reports, Lindsay's dad urged her to return to rehab. 'I think that Lindsay needs to find a place where God is paramount in her life. If that place is rehab, so be it.' Michael, himself a recovering alcoholic, insisted his daughter needed to clean up and ditch her so-called friends. 'The people around her are a negative influence.'

Lindsay took note of his advice and checked into the Promises rehab facility in Malibu. Her representatives pleaded with the press to respect their client's privacy. 'Lindsay admitted herself to an intensive medical rehabilitation facility on Memorial Day. Because this is a medical matter, it is our hope that the press will appreciate the seriousness of the situation and respect the privacy of Lindsay as well as the other patients receiving treatment at the facility.'

The actress confessed that, although she had thousands of friends, she often felt lonely. 'The real hard thing about LA is that it's all about one thing. Everyone always wants something. This industry is very lonely; I tend to get very lonely. When it's a

Sunday and no one's around, and you see no cars go by, it's a challenge.' She hoped her stint in rehab would help resolve those feelings.

Her fashion stylist Nate Newell paid the actress a visit, and reported, 'She's happy where she is and is just taking time to herself to learn and be OK. I've been in touch with her and she likes it. She just needs to be away from everyone and not get attacked by the paparazzi. She's doing really, really well. She probably should be there and it will be the best for her. I think now she's ready for it.'

Calum Best also flew out to visit Lindsay. However, she allegedly refused to return his calls. Only days before Lindsay had checked into rehab, a British tabloid published pictures of Calum in a 'drug-fuelled romp' with two prostitutes. The same article also alleged he was seeing the model Claire Evans behind Lindsay's back.

'She knew Calum was no angel but she felt humiliated when she heard what he had been up to just as she checked herself into rehab,' reported a friend. 'People close to her had been trying to tell her that dating Calum would bring down her image but she just wouldn't listen. That is until she saw the pictures of him with the hookers for her own eyes.'

On 2 July, Lindsay Lohan would celebrate her 21st birthday. Originally she had intended to celebrate the momentous occasion with an extravagant party.

However, following her car accident several drinks sponsors had pulled out of the event. Suddenly, a flash party no longer seemed appropriate. Lindsay had always been the party girl, but maybe all that was about to change. As she prepared to enter the adult world, it was time to clean up her act and find some balance.

'I'm going to go away out of the country,' she said. 'Do something fun and different. They won't find me. No one can get a picture of you on Turks and Caicos. I go there with my family and it's the perfect place to go with a guy.'

Attempting to keep a lower profile, Lindsay dutifully focused her attentions on work and getting better. Although she managed to steer clear of nightclubs, she was yet to quell her second addiction – shopping. On a number of occasions she was spotted browsing in LA boutiques wearing a new fashion accessory around her ankle. The heavy black bracelet, known as a Secure Continuous Remote Alcohol Monitor or SCRAM, was used to monitor Lindsay's alcohol intake.

When Lindsay finally checked out of rehab on 15th July, she agreed to wear her bracelet for the foreseeable future. She was sending out a message to the world: She was determined to get better. 'In part she is wearing the bracelet so there are no questions about her sobriety if she chooses to go dancing or dining in a place where alcohol is served,' her publicist told reporters. 'Lindsay is working hard on her sobriety and we are all supporting her.'

Slowly, over time, Lindsay was beginning to appreciate the simple things in life. 'I'm happiest when I'm just sitting,' she insisted. 'Or taking a walk in the woods. I recently went to a redwood forest with a friend and went on a hike. It was the most fun I've ever had.'

More than anything, Lindsay was now more honest with herself. She didn't profess to be an angel or a saint. But she was learning how to exercise self-control and confront difficult home truths – domestic violence, eating disorders and experimenting with pot were now realities she could comfortably live with. She hoped to pass that knowledge on to her younger fans.

Underneath the surface, however, Lindsay was still suffering. Nightclubs and drinking had been a big part of her life and she was faced with temptation at every turn. Unfortunately her resolve broke while out partying with friends, just days after she had been booked in connection with her drunken driving charge back in May. Lindsay had been released after posting a $30,000 bond. She was due back in court on 24th August.

Early on the morning of 24th July the police received a troubled phone call from the mother of

Lindsay's personal assistant Tarin, who told them she was trying to drive to the Santa Monica California police department because someone was chasing her.

When police finally arrived on the scene, they found Lindsay at the wheel of the car chasing Tarin's mum. The officers smelled alcohol on Lindsay's breath and demanded she take a sobriety test. At first she protested and was taken to the police station, where she was forced to have blood tests. As the officers read out the results, Lindsay buried her head in her lap. She was one-and-a-half times over the legal limit.

Worse still, officers discovered a white powdery substance in her jeans pocket. It was determined to be cocaine. Lindsay's life was crumbling around her. She was charged with two counts of driving under the influence, possession of cocaine, bringing a controlled substance into a jail facility, and driving on a suspended licence. The police took an unflattering mug shot of a tired and bleary-eyed Lindsay, which later appeared in the tabloids.

Later that morning, Lindsay was freed from the jail after posting $25,000 bail. But she wouldn't get off that lightly. At some point she would have to appear in court on account of her two drink driving charges for which she could face up to five years in prison if found guilty.

Her lawyer Blair Berk released a statement.

'Addiction is a terrible and vicious disease. Since Lindsay transitioned to outpatient care, she has been monitored on a SCRAM bracelet and tested daily in order to support her sobriety. Throughout this period, I have received timely and accurate reports from the testing companies. Unfortunately, late yesterday I was informed that Lindsay had relapsed. The bracelet has now been removed. She is safe, out of custody and presently receiving medical care.'

That night Lindsay was due to appear on the *Tonight With Jay Leno* show to promote her new film *I Know Who Killed Me*. In light of her circumstances, she cancelled. The comedian Rob Schneider stepped in at the eleventh hour, mocking Lindsay by turning up in drag. He wore an alcohol bracelet around his ankle, which actually turned out to be a flask he could swig from. Jay Leno also cracked a couple of jokes at Lindsay's expense, saying, 'You know, we had Lindsay Lohan booked for our show tonight, but apparently she was already "booked". I thought our competition was *Letterman* and *Nightline*, but it turns out its *Cops* and *America's Most Wanted*.'

It wasn't the first time an alcohol- and drugs-related incident had rocked the Lohan family. Lindsay's dad, who was still serving time for driving under the influence, admitted that he felt largely responsible for what had happened. 'Everyone around Lindsay, especially her parents, have a direct bearing on her life and I made some really stupid choices in my life,' he confessed. 'I made some mistakes and I can definitely identify with what she's going through.'

'I am sick over this,' Dina Lohan told TV show *Entertainment Tonight*. 'My children, my family, we are like prisoners in our own home because paparazzi is staked outside. Lindsay is in a safe place, and we are trying to strategically work out our next step. We are doing everything in our power in support of Lindsay, and I won't give up. This is my daughter, and we love her. We are waiting for the press frenzy to die down and leave her alone. And please respect our privacy.'

No one was quite sure what had happened that night. Lindsay's personal assistant had quit her job just hours before the incident took place. When her mother came to pick her up, Lindsay allegedly gave chase. Desperate to prove her innocence, Lindsay sent an email to Access Hollywood host Billy Bush. It was later published on the show's website. 'I am innocent … did not do drugs they're not mine,' she claimed. 'I was almost hit by my assistant Tarin's mum. I appreciate everyone giving me my privacy.'

She'd grown up quickly in the limelight and had tackled a number of obstacles along the way, but now Lindsay was about to face her biggest challenge to date. Her recent behaviour was hardly exemplary, but at least Lindsay was ready to address her problems like an adult.

No longer a teenage drama queen, this remarkable young woman already has a lifetime's worth of experience behind her. Just like Lindsay's new choice of adult script, there is no tidy conclusion to her story; those days of Disney smiles and happy endings are over. And that's a good thing. No more lies, no more secrets; take Lindsay Lohan at face value. As Dina once astutely remarked, everyone loves Lindsay because she's real. Amen to that.